Thomas Jackson's autobiography provides a colourful account of his experiences as a militiaman, Coldstreamer, and Chelsea pensioner.

Son of a Walsall buckle-maker, Jackson joined the Staffordshire Militia aged 17 and spent a decade on home service, much of it passed at Windsor Castle and Weymouth guarding King George III. As a sergeant in the Coldstream Guards, he served in Sir Thomas Graham's 1813-14 campaign in the Netherlands and was wounded and captured during the storming of Bergen-op-Zoom. Jackson provides a harrowing account of this failed assault, the ensuing amputation of his right leg, and his subsequent year-long convalescence. While many military memoirs end with news of peace or discharge, Jackson also chronicles his post-war life as a Chelsea pensioner and war amputee, describing his struggles raising a family amidst economic turmoil and cholera outbreaks.

Jackson offers a fresh and often critical perspective on service in the ranks. Embittered by the loss of his leg, he laments the plight of army veterans, doomed by an ungrateful nation to lives of 'pinching poverty'. His memoir also does not shrink from graphically describing the horrors of combat. Indeed, Neil Ramsey, author of a recent comprehensive study of military memoirs, wrote that Jackson's story deserved 'far wider attention as one of the most harrowing accounts of war's miseries to be written in the nineteenth century'.

Yet despite the clear merits of his testimony, Jackson's *Narrative* has never been reissued since its initial publication. Enhanced with additional research and commentary by historian Eamonn O'Keeffe, this new edition makes Jackson's lively and invaluable autobiography publicly available for the first time in 170 years.

Thomas Jackson (1785/6-1859) joined the Staffordshire Militia in 1803 and transferred to the Coldstream Guards in 1812. He lost his right leg at Bergen-op-Zoom in 1814 and was discharged with a pension from the Royal Hospital Chelsea. Jackson returned to Walsall, his home town, and later worked as a coal merchant's clerk, schoolteacher, and plater.

Eamonn O'Keeffe recently completed a degree in history at Merton College, Oxford. His research on British Napoleonic-era military music, courts-martial, and soldiers' memoirs has been published in *Canadian Military History* and the *Journal of the Society for Army Historical Research*. He served as Drum-Major of the Fort York Guard until 2016, leading a fife and drum corps at Canada's best-preserved War of 1812 historic site.

Narrative of the Eventful Life of Thomas Jackson

Militiaman and Coldstream Sergeant, 1803-15

Thomas Jackson, with New Introduction, Notes, and Commentary by Eamonn O'Keeffe

Helion & Company Limited

Helion & Company Limited
26 Willow Road
Solihull
West Midlands
B91 1UE
England
Tel. 0121 705 3393
Fax 0121 711 4075
Email: info@helion.co.uk
Website: www.helion.co.uk
Twitter: @helionbooks
Visit our blog at http://blog.helion.co.uk/

Published by Helion & Company 2018
Designed and typeset by Mach 3 Solutions Ltd (www.mach3solutions.co.uk)
Cover designed by Paul Hewitt, Battlefield Design (www.battlefield-design.co.uk)
Printed by Lightning Source Limited, Milton Keynes, Buckinghamshire

ISBN 978-1-912390-12-0

British Library Cataloguing-in-Publication Data.

A catalogue record for this book is available from the British Library.

Contents

List of Illustrations

List of Maps

New Introduction

By Eamonn O'Keeffe

Despite its clear merits as a historical source, the *Narrative of the Eventful Life of Thomas Jackson* has never been reissued since its original 1847 printing. Only a handful of copies survive in university and research libraries in the United Kingdom and North America; even the British Library only has a photocopy of the book.

Yet despite the relative inaccessibility of Jackson's memoir, numerous scholars over the years have recognized the *Narrative*'s value. Anthologized in Roy Palmer's classic *The Rambling Soldier*,[1] Jackson's prose has been cited widely in studies of military medicine and the English militia as well as general histories of the British Army and the Napoleonic Wars.[2] Neil Ramsey, who examined scores of soldiers' narratives in a recent monograph on the military memoir as a literary genre, singled out Jackson's story as meriting 'far wider attention as one of the most harrowing accounts of war's miseries to be written in the nineteenth century'.[3]

My interest piqued by scattered quotations in secondary sources, I ordered the photocopy of the *Narrative* from the closed stacks during a visit to the British Library and soon chanced on Jackson's fulsome description of John Lyster, the Staffordshire Militia's veteran drum-major. Owing to my longstanding interest in military music, I immediately connected this detailed pen-portrait with a painting

1 Roy Palmer, *The Rambling Soldier* (Gloucester: Sutton, 1985), pp. 24-8, 77-8, 254-7.

2 See for instance, Matthew McCormack, *Embodying the Militia in Georgian England* (Oxford: Oxford University Press, 2015), pp. 175, 182-3; Joanna Bourke, *The Story of Pain: From Prayer to Painkillers* (Oxford: Oxford University Press, 2014), pp. 270-1, 299-300; Michael Crumplin, *Men of Steel: Surgery in the Napoleonic Wars* (Shrewsbury: Quiller, 2007), pp. 122, 216; Richard Holmes, *Redcoat: The British Soldier in the Age of Horse and Musket* (London: HarperCollins, 2001), pp. 142, 260, 416, 419; Philip Haythornthwaite, *Redcoats: The British Soldiers of the Napoleonic Wars* (Barnsley: Frontline, 2012), pp. 172-3; Jenny Uglow, *In these Times: Living in Britain through Napoleon's Wars 1793-1815* (London: Faber & Faber, 2014), pp. 30, 32.

3 Neil Ramsey, *The Military Memoir and Romantic Literary Culture, 1780-1835* (Farnham: Ashgate, 2011), p. 198.

held by the National Army Museum in Chelsea, 'The Staffordshire Militia on parade at Windsor Castle' – the same image which now graces the cover of this book. Pleased though I was to have identified the drum-major featured in the painting, I could not help but conclude as I perused the memoir that Jackson's lively account of his 'eventful life' deserved a far wider audience.

However, readers hoping for tales of swashbuckling exploits and martial triumphs may be disappointed by the *Narrative*. After almost a decade of home service in the Staffordshire Militia, Jackson saw active duty abroad for scarcely three months as part of Sir Thomas Graham's relatively inglorious campaign in the Low Countries, his military career cut short by wounds received during the shambolic assault on Bergen-op-Zoom in March 1814. Although Jackson played no part in the more familiar Peninsular and Waterloo campaigns, his memoirs nonetheless offer many worthwhile insights for students of the British experience during the Napoleonic Wars. Besides accounts of service at Windsor Castle and in the Netherlands, Jackson provides invaluable descriptions of his subsequent travails as a prisoner of war, convalescent, and disabled veteran.

According to the author, the *Narrative* had not initially been intended for publication, but was penned as 'a record of my history' to bequeath to his children and their descendants. Yet with the assistance of local Yeomanry officer Captain John Forster, who read the manuscript, and the subscriptions of Walsall Masonic brethren, yeomanry members and 'fellow townsmen', Jackson was able to publish his account with the Birmingham printer Josiah Allen and Son.

Tinged with bitterness at the loss of his right leg, Jackson adopted an anti-war stance and rarely shrank from furnishing graphic details of combat and injury. Unlike better-known soldier-memoirists like Rifleman Benjamin Harris, who reflected on their military service with pride, Jackson ultimately felt degraded for having been a soldier, convinced he had been cast off by an ungrateful nation with a pittance for a pension.[4] But despite his sense of grievance, the veteran had no sympathy for contemporary political radicals, denouncing them as opportunists who exploited Britain's post-war economic desperation to spread 'dangerous and wrong-headed' ideas.

Jackson's account is also inevitably coloured by his mid-life religious awakening. As described in an appendix, although Jackson read the works of Paine and Voltaire and embraced 'anti-christian' Deism during his military service, he returned to the Anglican communion in the mid-1820s and became a fervent believer. The spiritual component of his *Narrative* is more subdued than in many other Napoleonic-era rankers' accounts, and Jackson does not directly credit

4 For a scholarly comparison of Harris' *Recollections* and Jackson's *Narrative*, see Neil Ramsey, '"A Real English Soldier": Suffering, Manliness and Class in the Mid-Nineteenth-Century Soldiers' Tale' in Catriona Kennedy and Matthew McCormack (eds), *Soldiering in Britain and Ireland, 1750-1850* (Basingstoke: Palgrave Macmillan, 2013), pp. 136-55.

his traumatic wartime experiences with inspiring his faith. Yet in retrospect the veteran expressed his debt to 'ever watchful Providence' for rescuing him from 'the jaws of death' at Bergen-op-Zoom, thereby sparing him to find peace and true religion in his native Walsall.

Jackson's recollections will be of special interest to students of Graham's campaign in the Low Countries or the Napoleonic-era English Militia. Although this publication is not the place for detailed analysis of either subject, I have provided information on both topics in the notes as an aid to uninitiated readers.

Those wishing to learn more about the wartime militia would do well to consult Matthew McCormack's recent *Embodying the Militia in Georgian England* or John Cookson's *The British Armed Nation, 1793-1815*, although J.R. Western's *The English Militia in the Eighteenth Century* remains a classic study.

Aspiring students of the 1813-14 Low Countries campaign are advised to refer to Andrew Bamford's *A Bold and Ambitious Enterprise*, the only substantial modern work on the subject in English. Readers looking for further personal narratives of the campaign to complement Jackson's memoir should consult *Old Stick Leg: Extracts from the Diaries of Major Thomas Austin*, the account of a 2/35th lieutenant published in 1926, and *Triumphs and Disasters: Eyewitness Accounts from the Netherlands Campaign, 1813-1814*, a recent collection of primary sources also edited by Andrew Bamford.

The text of Jackson's 1847 *Narrative* is presented here in full without emendation, although square brackets have been used occasionally to identify errors of spelling or syntax. Footnotes are employed throughout to identify people and places, clarify unfamiliar terms, and provide any supplementary information necessary to place the account in its proper context.

Researching and annotating this memoir has been a distinct pleasure, and I very much hope that readers find Jackson's *Narrative*, to borrow the Coldstream motto, to be *nulli secundus*.

Eamonn O'Keeffe
Cambridge, UK
December 2017

THIS NARRATIVE IS RESPECTFULLY DEDICATED

TO CAPTAIN JOHN FORSTER,

OF THE

QUEEN'S OWN ROYAL YEOMANRY

OF STAFFORDSHIRE,

A GENTLEMAN WHOSE NAME WILL EVER LIVE IN THE AUTHOR'S GRATEFUL REMEMBRANCE

Apology

My simple tale was not at first intended for publication, but at the suggestion of the gallant Captain Forster,[1] my chief patron, who had read the manuscript, and also at the request of other valued friends, I at length, in tremulous suspense, consented to encounter public criticism. Having no merit in my own esteem, I beg the patient forbearance of the well informed reader, in the humble hope that all who may peruse it will find it more interesting than I anticipate.

T. J.

1 Captain John Forster of the Queen's Own Royal Regiment of Staffordshire Yeomanry, Walsall Troop, was appointed Lieutenant on 20 December 1819 and Captain on 1 August 1839. See P.C.G. Webster, *Records of the Queen's Own Royal Regiment of Staffordshire Yeomanry* (Lichfield: Lomax, 1870), Appendix, pp. xvi, xviii and *passim*.

Preface

Although a man, being his own biographer, may be suspected of partiality, it is impossible for any other to write the life of a soldier, with truth, but the soldier himself. No one can trace him through the intricate maze in his chequered path. The moment he has taken the oath of fidelity, he becomes a separate and a distinct being from all other society. He lives, and moves, and has his existence in another sphere, as it were in another world. He has no power over himself. His every moving action is by stern command. Wherever he is, or whatever he does, he is as a living automaton. He has sold himself for a period—perhaps for life, to serve his country, which contract he ought to keep inviolate. And being so separated by the military laws and customs, he lives in obscurity to the civil world around him, both at home and abroad. But few are allowed to witness his mode of living and doings, or his treatment in his barrack, his camp, his cantonments, his bivouac, or his hospital. Therefore, no one can tell his tale but himself. I had no wish to tell mine, in all its harrowing details, but as a gratifying remembrancer to my children, and theirs, after I am no more.

I can say nothing of myself out of the ordinary way, during my juvenile days, with the exception of two incidents. The one, at ten years of age, I was severely burnt with gunpowder: the other, at fourteen, I was saved from drowning, when sliding on a fish-pond, then in Walsall vicarage grounds. Nothing further until, at the age of seventeen, when I entered the militia, from which period I commence my history.[1] That service, going over a space of several years, may not be very interesting, still it is necessary I should describe it, to show the nature of life in that corps; the duties and discipline required in time of war, which, though at home, are not altogether smooth affairs; likewise to shew the contrast between the quiet life of the soldier at

1 While the term 'militia' often conjures up mental images of Dad's Army amateurs, the English militia, established in 1757 to defend against French invasion during the Seven Years' War, was a full-time professional force in wartime, albeit one typically limited to 'home service' within the British Isles. County militia regiments, disembodied (i.e. demobilized) after the 1802 Peace of Amiens, were re-raised when war loomed once more the following year. Although, as Jackson later laments, the militia were sometimes derided as chocolate-box soldiers for their lack of battlefield experience, they were essential to Britain's war effort, freeing regular regiments for service abroad by bolstering home defence and performing tedious domestic duties like guarding enemy prisoners. The militia also proved a vital source of trained reinforcements for line regiments, helping replace losses suffered in overseas campaigns.

home, and the toilsome, whirlabout, and perilous life of the soldier serving abroad. My military career, occupying about twelve years of my life, after a certain period of promising sunshine, became a clouded, thorny path to march in, marked by a series of adversity and misfortune (painful to bring up into memory), such having resulted in the loss of a limb, the consequences of which, as may be supposed, have been a drag upon my affairs throughout my subsequent life. I have not borrowed from any, to enlarge or garnish my simple story, except to relieve a monotony, or, by an occasional anecdote, or jocular stroke, to raise a humorous ridicule.

All the incidents of my military life, pleasant or painful, I have given in succession, as they turned up, from beginning to end, without straining any point to embellish my tale, but leave it as original as memory would serve. Upon a review of the whole, it is still a wonder to myself how a human being could exist under such intense suffering from cold, loss of blood, barbarity of the enemy, and want of food, as I did, while a prisoner in Bergen-op-Zoom, and wounded; and, on my release, being, in bitter frost, drawn all night in a waggon without any covering; and afterwards, in the process of obtaining a cure, which occupied seventeen months, prior to my discharge. After that, persecuting fate seemed to consign me to a new series of troubles and adversities in civil life, marked, as will be seen, with a succession of untoward events, with but one bright interval of cheering prosperity, through my subsequent life of thirty years, in which it then pleased God to give me health, and strength, and prudence, to make the best use of. This is alluding to my having at length, though late in life, had the good fortune, through my own labours, to obtain the means of building myself a dwelling-house, wherein to cover my grey hairs.

A few years after this, my hard tried constitution began to give way; my health so much injured, I was forced, in my sixtieth year, to relinquish my business as a plater altogether. Being no longer able to work, I have amused myself in writing this narrative of my eventful life, in my sixty-second year. It has been written at various times, as health would permit, and often then under much debility, which, I hope, may claim the patience of the reader, to overlook errors and inaccuracies.

Thomas Jackson

To the Officers, Non-Commissioned Officers, and Privates of the Walsall Troop of the Queen's Own Royal Staffordshire Yeomanry, I have to offer my proud acknowledgments for their liberal support. Also the Brethren of the Masonic Lodge, 786, of Walsall (an honourable Order to which I belong, of Lodge 209), have my especial regard for their favours and never-to-be-forgotten kindness; and to my Fellow Townsmen of every grade, who have given so extraordinary a patronage to my narrative, I desire, in the most emphatic terms of respect, to convey my thanks for their willing response to my solicitation.

T.J.

1

Enlistment into the King's Own Staffordshire Regiment of Militia

Before commencing my militia narrative it will be necessary to state what I was prior to having entered into that service, and what induced me to enter.

A native of Walsall, in the county of Stafford, a town now famous for its numerous hardware manufactures, its extensive commerce, and mining interests.[1] A rapidly thriving and prosperous place in the time of regularity in trade: but the commerce of the country having, ever since I can remember, been subject to a sort of periodical panic, the working classes of this town have had to encounter much periodic privation and distress in consequence; and, without doubt, has driven many of my fellow townsmen to enter the army, who, under fairer circumstances, would never have enlisted. Many of whom are now to be seen old, worn out, emaciated, unable to labour, dragging out in pinching poverty the miserable remnant of life upon a small pension; though of course they have, as I have, such as was then allowed by Act of Parliament.

My father, Thomas Jackson, a native also of Walsall, was a manufacturer of all sorts of japanned and polished shoe and other iron and steel buckles: a very profitable trade in its day of prosperity.[2] He was an honest, upright, and hard working man; always anxiously endeavouring for the welfare of his family, which consisted

1 Located eight miles north-west of Birmingham in Staffordshire, Walsall had a population of 10,399 at the 1801 census. During Jackson's life Walsall underwent rapid transformation from a market town to a leading industrial centre in the West Midlands. As he suggests, metalworking and coal mining were among Walsall's principle economic pursuits. For a nineteenth-century guide to the town, see *Ancient and Modern History of the Borough of Walsall...* (Walsall: J.L. Chavasse, 1838).

2 The son of Thomas and Elizabeth Jackson, Thomas Jackson was christened on 27 March 1786 at St Matthew's Parish Church in Walsall, Staffordshire. The 1801 census lists Thomas Jackson Senior as a buckle manufacturer living in Dudley Street, Walsall. See Ann French, *Thomas Jackson: A Walsall soldier in the Napoleonic Wars* (Local Lives No. 2, Walsall Local History Centre, 1993), p. 3 and 'Population of the Township of the Borough of Walsall, taken May 1801...by one Thomas Pearce, one of the Overseers of the Poor', ref Acc. 277/245/1, Walsall Local History Centre. Transcript available at <https://go.walsall.gov.uk/Portals/0/images/importeddocuments/walsall_census_1801_transcript.pdf> (accessed 11 October 2017).

'A North-West View of Walsall in 1795, from a drawing by Reverend S. Shaw'. (Public Domain)

of five sons and one daughter. I was the second son of the five. We were brought up to the established church, and had a common share of education, merely to qualify us for business, and all of us that were then able were being brought up to my father's trade; the articles of which were chiefly for export to Germany, Holland, France, and Spain. But owing to the long protracted war with several of those countries, our trade became nearly lost, and, consequently, impoverished my father with so heavy a family, and, with all, provisions at that time were at a famine price: it may be seen on record, that awhile before the Peace of 1802, flour was from twenty-seven to thirty shillings the bushel; potatoes, two shillings and sixpence per peck; the quartern loaf, one shilling and ten-pence halfpenny, and all other eatables in equivalent proportion. However, peace being made, my father's prospects of trade began to brighten up, and threw a cheering hope over the gloom behind. But, alas! fallacious hope was too short lived to do us any permanent good. Destructive, ruinous war, was again proclaimed against France, in May 1803. Trade now quite stagnated, and nothing but starvation was looked for by the working classes. I used to see my mother always weeping, and my father always grieving. I was then seventeen years of age; old enough to feel for the distressed condition of my parents, and wished I had the means to alleviate their distress. As we had nothing to do, my brothers turned out to seek some other employment: I believed such would be fruitless so far as concerned myself. About this time a balloting for the militia had commenced, and under a delusion held out to young men that the calling-out would only be for twenty-eight days training and then home again I, with other youngsters, resolved to enlist, as a substitute for a drawn man.[3] My father's grief had brought upon him a fever which confined him to his bed, and which continued for a long time. I thought, by this act, whether judicious or not – I had taken it at the risk upon myself – still by this means I could help my parents a little in their necessity. My enlistment was not known to my parents: I had told no one, lest that event should grieve my father, as I was his favourite son. I had been missing three days, meanwhile they supposed I had gone after my brothers to seek employ. However, I had been taken to Stafford, to be enrolled and sworn in, or attested. When I returned home, my imprudence, as my mother called it, gave some uneasiness on that account. I had received a small bounty of six pounds; and, as I had never been used to having money of my own, more than a shilling, I thought this a great sum. I then went to my poor father's sick bed, and presented him with half of my bounty; he wept at our hard lot, and gave me his blessing. I then took my leave to join the assembling regiment at Stafford. So now I have just taken the first step, lucky or unlucky, into the incidental life of a soldier, in the character of a militia man.[4]

This sort of soldier, who must do all that he is commanded to do, and may have merit in his sphere, is always the subject of taunt and ridicule of the soldier of the line, who gives him the soft and easy title of the "feather bed soldier;" true, he may have a bed of some kind when he is off duty, though it be *long feathers*, while the man of war abroad may not have [any]where to lay his head; but when in England their duties and discipline are just the same. The militia man being the home soldier, he engages to go no farther than Ireland at the most, while the soldier of the marching regiment of the line must go the world over, if he is so ordered. But after all, be it said to the man of war, as there is no inferiority in the comparison when at home, the only difference in point of character is, the desperate gallantry, or savage ferocity, the line man obtains in the battle, and the rough hardihood he acquires from being exposed to wind and weather night and day, bad lodgings, and other want of comforts; for such things as these are common to the soldier in time of war. Now with these exceptions, if taken from such a regiment as I was trained in, "The King's Own, Stafford," the militia soldier is, in every point of order and discipline, not only his equal, but, perhaps, his superior. For instance, marching regiments are so frequently on the move, to and from foreign quarters –having no settled place long together, even at home – so that they have not the means of being made very perfect in their discipline. While the militia regiments

3 The English militia was organized with a degree of compulsion; able-bodied men aged 18 to 45 were liable to be balloted for service. However, this fell short of outright conscription as many categories of men (including clergy, sailors and apprentices) were exempt and balloted civilians unwilling to serve could avoid militia duty by hiring substitutes to serve in their stead. Indeed, the majority of militiamen, including Jackson, were not balloted men but volunteers paid to take the place of others.

4 Jackson's pension record gives his date of enlistment in the Staffordshire Militia as 3 May 1803. However, Jackson is listed as serving from 11 March 1803 in the re-embodied regiment's monthly pay lists. See The National Archives (TNA), WO 97/181/59 and WO 13/1949, 1803 Staffordshire Militia Pay Lists.

are usually located in one spot for years together, and kept in constant drill and field practice till they attain the highest degree of discipline: hence the more than probable superiority. And, farther, it may be observed, that in the first several years of the late French War, our troops made but few conquests, but oftener sustained defeat, owing, in all probability, to want of well trained men; it being, to my knowledge, the custom to raise recruits as fast as possible, and, with scarcely any drill at the home depot, send them off to fight when they must be defective. But observe, again, the difference after the militias had been out and practised all sorts of duties for seven or eight years, and encouraged by large bounties to volunteer by thousands into the line, then we heard scarcely of any thing but victories, down to the close of the war. So now where is the boast over the militia man? The militia soldier, too, is governed by the same martial law as he of the line; the Mutiny Act, or Articles of War, are read to him every month, and for any breach of these articles he is equally liable to punishment, as the act reads, almost at the end of every clause – "he shall suffer death or such other punishment as by a general or regimental court martial shall be awarded."

But to return from vindicating the merits of the militia soldier. I had now arrived at Stafford, the head quarters of this afterwards highly favoured regiment, in the esteem of royalty. Every public house was crammed with its number of men. I felt very much disappointed in the new society I had now to live among. I could form no companionship after my own way; I found the young men generally lamentably ignorant, ill-behaved, and given to drinking. I had never been in a pothouse to drink before;[5] neither did their ridicule tempt me to begin. For the first week all was stir and bustle; commencing drill, and being fitted out with regimental uniform. I now saw myself a new figure – my head being trimmed to order, and crimped with hot irons; my blood red coat, white small-belows,[6] with black leggings; belted and armed; and with a long leather cue, or tail, fastened to my pole.[7] A strange metamorphosis, thought I, of myself, since the day before. Now I had nothing to do but reconcile myself to these awkward habiliments, to make them fit easy.

The painful task of drill exercises was now to be performed, for six or eight hours every day, until the end of the twenty-eight days, when we were expecting to return home. But lo! to our chagrin and surprise, a Government order and route was received to march us off to Windsor; and so peremptory was it, that no time was allowed to see friends. However, a little reflection soon reconciled me to this movement. Having never been from home, I now felt pleased at the idea of seeing

5 Pothouse: a tavern.

6 Small-belows: breeches. The term 'small-belows' presumably refers to the fact these short trousers were fastened at the small or hollow below the knee-cap.

7 Hair queues were abolished in the army by a general order of 20 July 1808. Thenceforth, soldiers wore their hair short and unpowdered.

'View of a street in Coventry with the King's Head Inn and Peeping Tom' by Thomas Rowlandson. From H. Wigstead, *Remarks on a Tour to North and South Wales, in the Year 1797.* (London: Wigstead, 1800)

the country through which we had to pass; but more especially the celebrated Windsor Castle, the residence of so many kings, and now of George the Third, where we were going to be honoured in doing duty.[8] With these thoughts, I was desirous of beginning this my first march, but little dreaming, while anticipating its pleasurable results, what should in years after be the result of my last march – the loss of a leg.

The march commenced; and from the progress we had made during our twenty-eight days' drill exercises, we were enabled to move off with a something like soldierly appearance. Our route lay through Lichfield and Coventry, and so on upwards. It always was my custom, after marching into a town, to clean myself and view it over; and with what other means I had, to regard the customs and manners of the people, for such things were not only amusing, but edifying. I was highly gratified with the view of the magnificent cathedral of Lichfield; I

8 The Staffordshire Militia's close association with King George III began in 1797, when the monarch, impressed by the regiment's fine appearance and fervently expressed loyalty to the Crown, invited the corps to take up royal duties at Windsor Castle, his main residence. The regiment was frequently stationed there until it was disembodied following the 1802 Peace of Amiens. The corps was re-embodied the following year before war broke out again and received an order to return to Windsor Castle on 17 March 1803. See C.H. Wylly et al, *Historical Records of the 1st King's Own Stafford Militia* (Lichfield: Johnson's Head, 1902), pp. 11-14, and Thomas Fernyhough, *Military Memoirs of Four Brothers* (London: Joseph Masters, 1838), pp. 278-9.

think it excels all of the kind I have seen since. In marching to Coventry, and as we drew near the city, I thought of Falstaff marching his awkward and ragged regiment through,[9] and said, "Surely the people of Coventry cannot draw the ludicrous comparison between our new-fledged corps and that of Sir John's, although all recruits, and some awkwardness be discovered in our ranks?" Here I saw the celebrated Peeping Tom, of ancient notoriety, but regarded him with little interest, and so bid him good bye.[10] About six more days brought us to within one stage of now desired Windsor; I think it was High Wickham [sic – High Wycombe]. Here we had particular orders to assemble next morning, very neat and clean, as His Majesty the King was to ride out and meet us. This I thought great honour indeed. However, so it was for as we approached a small village called Salt Hill, about a mile and a half from Windsor, the king appeared, with his few attendants on horseback, to welcome his favourite Stafford regiment. This favouritism, I believe, arose out of the long and intimate attachment between the king and the then Earl of Uxbridge, who was the head colonel.[11]

Here we were halted for about half an hour, while the officers were paying their homage to His Majesty. Now, indeed, I thought myself highly privileged, to see and be so near the king, and to hear him talk. But here another interesting object had taken my attention. From this spot the noble and majestic castle of Windsor, the chief residence of royalty, was charmingly conspicuous. I was delighted with the magnificent view of its lofty colossal towers of white stone; its turrets, its eminence above the town, together with its sloping shrubbery from the northern terrace, down some hundred yards, into the deer park below, which is skirted by the noble Thames, formed altogether, to my novice mind, a scene unparalleled. I promised myself the future pleasure of minutely surveying both the exterior and interior of this wonderful massive pile, so far as I might be permitted, and, verily, it so happened, during our long stay at Windsor, that I had my gratification to the full. My duties, day and night, for a long time (at least once a week), were always in or about this interesting royal castle; so that in the course of my duties and leisure together, I had ample time and opportunity to view it, even to telling

9 The fictional comic knight Sir John Falstaff appears in several of Shakespeare's plays. In Act 4, Scene 2 of *Henry IV, Part I*, Falstaff delivers a monologue excoriating his motley band of ill-trained recruits and jailbirds while on the road to Coventry. References to Falstaff's 'ragged regiment' are common in Napoleonic-era British military memoirs.

10 Peeping Tom, according to legend, was the only person to spy on Lady Godiva when she rode through Coventry naked in an effort to free the town from her husband's oppressive taxation. Jackson is referring to a seventeenth-century wooden effigy of Peeping Tom once prominently displayed near the King's Head Inn. The head and shoulders of the statue survive and remain on display in Coventry's Cathedral Lanes Shopping Centre.

11 Henry Bayley-Paget, 1st Earl of Uxbridge (1744-1812) served as colonel of the Staffordshire Militia from 1783 until his death. His son, the 2nd Earl of Uxbridge (later 1st Marquess of Anglesey), famously lost his right leg at Waterloo. See Wylly et al, *Historical Records*, p. 9, and *Oxford Dictionary of National Biography (ODNB).*

Map 1 Jackson's home service in England.

the stones in the ponderous towers; and not only so, but being favourites at that time at court, we were permitted, on certain days, by three at a time, into the state rooms, to view the magnificence of their ancient furniture, consisting of massive silver tables, chairs, and other articles; Queen Anne's state bed, with steads of solid gold; statuary; and immense numbers of ancient arms and other implements used in war, in the olden time, very interesting. This princely residence of our gracious sovereign occupies several acres of land, standing on a lofty eminence above the town, yet the lower part of it communicates with the town. No one can form a just estimate of the edifice without having seen it, nor am I well able to describe it properly. The upper court, or quadrangle, as it, is called, but which I call an oblong square, is very spacious, so that our regiment and another of cavalry (on foot) used to form in rank, all round the oblong, every Sunday morning, for the king to look at. On every Sunday, too, twelve men from each regiment had always to attend divine service, at St. George's Chapel, with His Majesty.

In the upper court is the king's residence, the queen's, and others of the various branches of the royal family, occasionally.[12]

12 The Upper Ward of Windsor Castle still houses the monarch's private apartments as well as the State Apartments, which are now open to the public.

'Queen Anne's Bed – Windsor Castle'. Print from W.H. Pyne, *The History of the Royal Residences*, Vol. I. (London: Dry, 1819)

Of the towers, the chief and grandest is called the Round Tower, or Keep; this is fortified with a battery of guns, near the top, and has an exceedingly deep ditch at its base. From the top of this high tower the guide points out eleven different counties. The tower, besides, is filled with ancient arms and armour. Among the vast and noble buildings of the castle are St. George's Chapel, of exquisite grandeur, both exterior and interior; the Royal Mausoleum, a church; the residences of the Archbishop of Canterbury and several bishops; the cloisters for the dean and canons; the residences of knights of various Orders, high military officers, &c.; and is guarded day and night by about one hundred soldiers. This description applies chiefly to the period of the latter part of the reign of George the Third, but many improvements have been made since then during the reigns of George the Fourth and William the Fourth.

From this digression I return to Salt Hill. The king had returned to Windsor; and now the word is given to finish this *long* march, as I thought it. Headed by the old and well trained band, and with flying colours, we entered the town, welcomed by the inhabitants, but who looked upon us as the "awkward squad," compared with the old Stafford regiment they had there a year or two before. Now we enter

'The Upper Ward – Windsor Castle'. Print from W.H. Pyne, *The History of the Royal Residences*, Vol. I. (London: Dry, 1819)

the large and spacious foot barracks, perhaps the finest and best built in the kingdom.[13] Over the centre is placed, in large stone figures, the national arms. While we were standing in the yard, some of the young ones began to lark each other, when they were called to order by the surly old sergeant-major, who pointed up to the lion and unicorn, saying, "Do you see that?" "Yes, sir." "Then that's the sign of *the case is altered*!"[14] I took the hint and never forgot it after. The look of this man was a terror to me for some time, until I got used to him.

And now I should just like to describe him. He was of gigantic stature, big boned and limbed, measuring in height about six feet two inches, and, probably, then about fifty years of age; rather corpulent; a fine full red face; a piercing eye; nose aquiline, well set to match with full cheeks, one of which was usually a little more prominent than the other, caused by the introduction of a delicious "plum" of tobacco. Now this may raise a smile, but let it be called the insignia of the old weather beaten soldier or sailor in long service. And with his Stentorian voice he

13 These 'handsome and commodious barracks', according to contemporary travel guides, were erected in Sheet Street in 1795 and enlarged in 1803. See *The Windsor Guide, containing a description of the Town and Castle...* (Windsor: Knight & Son, 1819), p. 27.

14 This legal proverb, analogous to saying 'circumstances have changed', was coined by English lawyer Sir Edmund Plowden (1518-1585). The maxim was also the title of a 1609 comedy by Ben Jonson and lives on as the namesake of several English pubs. Note that although Jackson employs the modern spelling of sergeant here, the older alternative serjeant is also used interchangeably throughout the text.

'The Staffordshire Militia on parade at Windsor Castle', c. 1804, circle of Arthur William Devis. (1763-1822) (National Army Museum)

used to make us young chaps tremble.[15] Such a figure may be supposed, when dressed in his enormous cocked hat, large white bullion epaulettes, broad belt, sash, and long boots, would be a fine noble fellow; and so he was, and an excellent disciplinarian. Though I then called him surly, I afterwards found him no tyrant, but a very good man. He was also a great favourite of the king: so much so that the king had his picture painted as he stood at guard-mounting, and had it placed in the castle.[16] And, more than that, in two or three years after His Majesty made him a gentleman, and took him into the castle to perform some little office about his person; to the honour of Staffordshire for producing such a man. His name was Cooper.[17]

15 Stentorian: loud or powerful in sound. This adjective, common in Napoleonic-era military memoirs, references Stentor, the legendary Greek herald in the Trojan War whose voice was described in the *Iliad* as equal to those of fifty men.

16 This may well refer to the painting, 'The Staffordshire Militia on parade at Windsor Castle', circle of Arthur William Devis, c. 1804, now held by the National Army Museum.

17 Long-time sergeant-major of the Staffordshire Militia, John Cooper was discharged on 7 September 1808. See TNA, WO 13/1954, 1808 Pay Lists. No further references could be found to his subsequent royal service at Windsor Castle.

While speaking of majors minor, I wish to introduce yet one other – the major of drums; especially as there are yet living some of his children, who will read this and see their father; he was a curious character – a very old soldier, who had, when young, served in the line. Although more than sixty, he had the agility of a boy; his person rather tall, finely erect, and proportionate – the very pink of a soldier. His countenance [was] fine, fresh and fixed, and [he] had the eye of an eagle. He would never turn his head about, but his eye. Extremely droll and witty in leisure moments, prior to parade falling in, the serjeants would gather round him to hear his cramp sayings, till ready to drop with laughter – but not a muscle of his face would move; woe be to him who dared provoke him to a sarcastic cut; he would make him writhe, and heap the laughter of all upon him. The officers delighted to get him into the mess-room after dinner, when he would either bewilder them with his astounding legendary [sic], or stupify them with laughter. His dress, very conspicuous, was a long yellow coat, white bullion epaulettes, cocked hat, and red feather. When at a review in the little park, the regiment moving in slow march past the king, he, leading the band, would, in his salute, fix his eagle eye full on His Majesty's face, and, with a most extraordinary dexterity in changing his fine ornamented staff from one hand to the other by a peculiar flourish, never failed to make the king laugh.[18] He was facetiously called by the soldiers The Old Proud Canary. He died, and had a pompous funeral; the lodge of Free Masons in full costume as mourners, and followed by all the officers of the regiment to his last home. He was a Lichfield man, and his name was Lyster.[19]

The best men were now selected for the king's duties, and I now began to think of learning to soldier in good earnest; knowing that nothing less than a right line of good conduct would avail, I resolved to pursue it. I did so, and such conduct did not go long unrewarded by promotion.

18 George III had an apparent partiality for drum-majors. As George Thomas Landmann of the Royal Engineers recalled with evident disapproval, the King 'was notorious for invariably taking more notice of the drum-major's salutes… than [those] of any other person.' When for example the Drum-Major of the 1st Somerset Militia 'flourished his dazzling silver, balloon-headed cane' and saluted His Majesty, the King doffed his cap in melodramatic fashion but greeted the regiment's actual officers with merely 'a slight and hasty touch of his hat'. See G.T. Landmann, *Adventures and Recollections of Colonel Landmann*, vol. II (London: Colburn and Co., 1852), pp. 319-21.

19 Born in London c. 1732 and a shoemaker by trade, John Lyster served for twenty-five years in the 59th Foot before being discharged for rheumatism in 1780. He later served as the Staffordshire Militia's long-time drum-major, dying at age seventy-nine on 30 March 1811 as 'the senior drum-major in the army'. Thomas Fernyhough, a junior officer in the regiment, also offered a description of Lyster: 'He was highly distinguished in the service, by the peculiar elegance of his salute, which, added to his veteran appearance, and martial air, excited general admiration, and he was highly respected and regarded in the regiment for the integrity of his character.' See TNA, WO 120/8, 121/162/234; *The Monthly Magazine*, vol. 31, Part I for 1811 (London: Richard Phillips, 1811), p. 496; Fernyhough, *Military Memoirs of Four Brothers*, p. 280.

The drill and field exercises now began afresh with vigorous alacrity. Being now under the eye of royalty and a strict general, great restriction was laid upon all our doings. However, in a newly embodied regiment, it must be a work of time and severity to bring it up to the height of discipline necessary to such duties as those required at Windsor. After about three months' experience at this town, many of the men were found to be incorrigibly bad characters, which nothing but strong coercion could restrain. However, the punishments adopted were strong enough to subdue the most reprobate: awarding some to three or four weeks in the black hole, some to the "porcupine drill," as it is called, others to flogging, and, in some instances, to transportation. These punishments were for such as desertion, drunkenness, striking a superior officer, theft, neglect of duty, &c. The porcupine drill is very painful: the serjeant makes the man fix his bayonet – then present, as though to fire – in this painful position he marches him up and down for two hours at a time, eight hours a day, perhaps, for a month. Some deserted rather than endure it, but were always taken and brought back, and then flogged. The lieutenant-colonel was an old soldier, and very severe, determined to have discipline to the height.[20]

The first flogging I saw was for desertion; an awful sight to look upon. The process was thus: three halberts are set up; the heads are then tied together, and the bottom of the shafts are set outward until they form a firm triangle. Another halbert is then tied across the two in front breast high; and a fifth is fastened across at the small of the leg, to which the legs are tied. The hands are buckled together at the wrist, then a cord is run between them by which the arms are drawn up to the full stretch, and the cord fastened to the head of the halberts. The culprit is finally arraigned for flogging, and to receive, probably, three hundred lashes with the cat-o'-nine-tails. The doctor stands by; the commanding officer then gives order to the drummer to go on. The drummer, with his shirt sleeves turned up, strikes on one spot – the shoulder blade – with all his might; if he does not, the drum-major at his back beats him with his cane till he strikes harder. Each drummer gives fife-and-twenty lashes in turn. The first round generally brings a stream of blood to the waist; and as each proceeds to strike on the same spot, the mangled flesh will adhere to the lash, steeped in blood; some of the drum-boys being short trail the bloody cat in the gravel of the yard, which adds to the cut of every stroke. The poor victim, writhing in inconceivable agony, cries for mercy, but the answer is generally, "No," and, as I have heard added, "If I forgive you God will not forgive me: go on, drummer." The man faints; the doctor examines him, gives him water,

20 Walter Sneyd (1752-1829) was the long-time lieutenant-colonel of the Staffordshire Militia and had served as Member of Parliament for Castle Rising between 1784 and 1790. He first joined the regiment when it was re-embodied in 1776 during the American Revolutionary War and retired as 'Father of the Regiment' in April 1805 to 'universal regret.' His family's estate and manor house, Keele Hall, form the basis of the modern-day Keele University campus near Newcastle-under-Lyme. See Wylly et al, *Historical Records*, p. 15, and *History of Parliament Online.*

and if he revives, "Go on again," till he is exhausted. He is then taken down, and, with his coat thrown loosely over his shoulders, he is made to walk, perhaps half a mile, to the hospital. The cats are made of nine strong whip cords, each knotted up from the end, and a short stick for the handle. The first man I saw flogged was at Windsor barracks; the sight made me turn sick; I nearly dropped down. Many of the youths fainted and fell flat down.[21] This is sharp work now going on here, thought I to myself; this is truly "the sign of the case is altered." However, after a few years of these severities, and other restraints upon the disorderly, the regiment became perfected in the highest state of discipline; perhaps, none equal; a pattern of militias.

The king reviewed us before the first year was out, and was pleased to speak well of our soldierlike appearance, and the progress made. After this, having other duties to do by detachment at Kew, Epsom, and Hungerford, I was sent with the one to Kew. Here I innocently got into trouble, and narrowly escaped being flogged. The detachment consisted of about sixty men, a captain and a lieutenant. I was on guard at the king's palace.[22] After coming off sentry towards evening, an old soldier, one of the guard, induced me to go over the river Thames, close by, in the ferry boat, to see the town of Brentford. He said we could be back in an hour. I did not know the consequence of leaving the guard, readily complied, and went over. We might have been back in the hour, but the ferry boat had broken loose in a squall, and drifted, so that we had to go above a mile to a bridge, and then a mile more to the guardhouse. Meanwhile it was dark, and the captain had been to visit the guard, it being a sergeant's guard, and found that we were absent. At length we arrived; we were instantly made prisoners, marched up to the small barracks, and confined, at the same time ordered to be prepared to be marched prisoners to head quarters. However, next morning, when the escort was made ready to move us off, the captain sent for us. The lieutenant happened to belong to my company (the Light Infantry), and knowing my conduct before, made intercession for me, and begged me off from being sent prisoner, and thus saved me a certain flogging. So,

21 Soldiers compelled to watch floggings often recalled fainting or becoming sick. Lieutenant John Le Couteur of the 104th Foot 'fainted away like a Sick girl' when the swinging cat-o-nine-tails spattered his face with blood during one man's punishment while Private John Green of the 68th remembered feeling 'very ill' on witnessing a flogging for the first time: 'indeed several of my comrades fainted away'. See Donald E. Graves (ed.), *Merry Hearts Make Light Days: The War of 1812 Journal of Lieutenant John Le Couteur, 104th Foot* (Montreal: Robin Brass, 2012), p. 81, and John Green, *Vicissitudes of a Soldier's Life* (Louth: Jackson, 1827), p. 15.

22 This was Kew Palace on the south bank of the River Thames in Richmond, just upriver from London. Construction began on a Gothic-style 'Castellated Palace' at Kew under George III in 1801, but the still-unfinished structure, plagued by delays and spiraling costs, was eventually demolished by George IV in 1827. Other parts of the palace complex, including the seventeenth-century Dutch House, survive within Kew Gardens and may be visited.

with a severe reprimand from the captain, me one extra guard and the old soldier two, we got out of this scrape. This was a salutary warning to me ever after.[23]

After our return to head quarters things went on pretty smooth with me; the duty, though very strict, was not very hard. I took delight at length in my calling, and was always to be found cleaning my appointments, or reading such books as my slender means would furnish. I was not for the pothouse, as almost all my comrades were. The company to which I belonged, probably a hundred strong, were all picked men, full of life and health, but such a mass of ignorance and heathenism I could not have conceived to have been drawn together from our county. I had been brought up to the Church of England, and used to reading good books, but had any book of a religious character been seen in my hand, I should be sure of their scorn and derision. No thought ever taken about the soul's welfare; no instruction given at that time *by command*; but the army since is better regulated for the soldier's good. All the provision made was merely half an hour's prayers, read by a minister of the church on the big drum head, in the barrack yard, every Sunday morning. However, I continued my way – they went theirs. This brings me to about the close of the first year of my military life.

As I have promised to tell the soldier's life in his barrack, suffice it briefly told. Some barracks are very comfortable, and others are not so. The best I ever saw were those at Windsor; a palace compared with many others. Windsor barracks will hold about eight hundred men; the building is four stories high. The rooms are spacious; those on the ground floor take in two companies of men, probably ninety each, rank and file. The sergeants haye separate rooms. The men's rooms serve for mess, sitting, and sleeping rooms. Below (same size) is their cleaning room. The sleeping rooms each hold twenty-nine beds. The attics were appropriated to married soldiers. The rooms were kept remarkably clean and rubbed bright. Drum beats to rise at six in summer, and turn out. Each bed is folded, and sheets and blankets also laid in neat folding pleats. Knapsacks are neatly packed, and hung on pegs over the bed. The arms stand in a rack by the bedside. It was pretty to see the neatness and uniformity of these rooms. But, by the bye, no breakfast is got for the soldier at nine: the mess-drum beats at twelve. When I first went there I used to think that drum the most joyful music I ever heard. The mess was half a pound of boiled meat per man, a can of broth, and a pound of bread; he might either eat it or save it for supper. Two cooks cut out each man's mess on a coarse brown plate. An officer attends to see all seated at table, and a corporal, pointing to a mess, will ask, "Who shall have this?" A man, with his back turned, replies – naming one.[24]

23 Jackson is noted as 'Detached at Kew' in the regimental pay lists for 25 January to 24 February 1804. The lieutenant mentioned was either William Wilkinson or John Dutton Colt, there being two lieutenants at that time in Jackson's company. See TNA, WO 13/1950, 1804 Staffordshire Militia Pay Lists.

24 This messing procedure was meant to ensure fairness, giving every man an equal chance of receiving a choice or gristly cut of meat. See for instance Richard Holmes, *Redcoat: The British Soldier in the Age of Horse and Musket* (London: HarperCollins, 2001), p. 281.

Perhaps a bony mess will sometimes fall to the lot of an unlucky hungry one, when any thing but pleasant looks are shewn; however, the pump makes up the deficiency. Now the dinner drum and fife always played the tune of "O the Roast Beef of Old England,"[25] but it was "all gammon," for I never tasted a bit of roast till the Jubilee, at the cost of "the good old king."[26] After dinner – romps, foolish talk, and corrupting each other. Tattoo beating at nine. All in barracks, and roll call; every man standing at his bed, and his name on the foot. The full pay of a private is one shilling and a penny per day, to find him meat, drink, washing, shirts, shoes, stockings, and sundry other things. The diet was well adapted to keep us from growing too corpulent and inactive.

During the next several years I have not to particularize events so minutely as in the first, until I come to my leaving the militia, and entering into the Second Foot Guards, more generally called The Coldstream Guards.[27] It seemed to have been the custom of King George the Third to retire to that beautiful watering place, Weymouth, in Dorsetshire, to make his usual aquatic excursions on the smooth surface of the fine harbour, and so on, for several hours together, in his open state barge, or yacht.[28] He had his favourite Staffordshire regiment always to attend him. In the month of August this year (1804), we were ordered to march for Weymouth – about six days' stages. Nothing remarkable occurred on the way. When we arrived we had to pitch our tents on a rising ground, about half a mile from the town, in the stubble of a corn field, which, in wet weather, proved to be very bad lodging and footing. I was pleased enough at the novelty of a camp, and the idea of living in a tent, until I found the difference to that of barrack lodging. Fifteen men had to sleep in each of those little round canvass houses, where there was not sufficient room to lie down but in misery. The head rested against the canvass wall, and the feet were all mingled together round the pole in the centre.

25 The tune 'The Roast Beef of Old England' was written by Henry Fielding for his play *The Grub Street Opera*, first performed in 1731, and was adopted by the British Army as the 'Dinner Call' played by fifers and drummers to summon soldiers for their early afternoon meal. See, for instance, Samuel Potter, *The Art of Playing the Fife…* (London: Potter, 1817), p. 16.

26 King George III's Golden Jubilee, held on 25 October 1809, celebrated the beginning of the monarch's fiftieth year on the throne.

27 Officially, the Coldstream Guards are not referred to as the Second Foot Guards, in contrast to the Grenadier and Scots Guards which were numbered historically as the 1st and 3rd Foot Guards respectively. Although the Coldstream are second in seniority amongst the infantry regiments, the corps is in fact ten years older than the first-ranked Grenadier Guards, tracing its origins to 1650. The Coldstream refusal to concede their second-place status is reflected by their motto *Nulli Secundus* – Second to None. See Sir J.F.G. Ross-of-Bladensburg, *A History of the Coldstream Guards, from 1815 to 1895* (London: Innes & Co, 1895), p. 90.

28 George III made fourteen visits to Weymouth, a popular seaside resort town in Dorset, between 1789 and 1805 in the hopes of improving his health. The royal yacht, the *Royal Sovereign*, was launched in 1804, replacing a smaller vessel, the *Royal Charlotte*, that had been used for the King's earlier Weymouth excursions. For additional information, see Alan Chedzoy, *Seaside Sovereign: King George III at Weymouth* (Dorset: Dovecote, 2003).

Some straw was littered on the ground, the knapsack served for a pillow, and each man had a blanket to cover him. All our arms and accoutrements were fastened to hooks round the pole. The tents were set in rows, forming regular streets, and was a pleasing sight from a short distance. The cooking kitchens stood in the rear, curiously formed of banked up earth. An enormous gun fired at daybreak, from a lofty eminence; though a mile off its flash penetrated through our tents long before hearing the report. Then would the isolated military world around be roused by the general beating of réveillie. This was camp in England.

The situation was very pleasant in fine weather, having a commanding view of the sea and shipping. Being young and hearty, the sea breeze made me so hungry that I wanted double the quantity of food my pay and allowances afforded me. Two other regiments were encamped in the adjacent fields, besides a regiment of heavy German cavalry in a barrack,[29] and, withal, the duty was very hard; we had so much field practice, and so many fatiguing night guards and picquets to perform. These picquets were sent off in large bodies of men, to various stations along the sea coast, seven or more miles from Weymouth; and sentries were posted along for miles, to prevent any surprise, by the enemy landing to take the king. A curious occurrence happened about this time, between myself and a German soldier. The first time I was sent out on one of these picquets, my turn for sentry happening about midnight, I was posted half a mile from the picquet-house, near the sea, on a common, middle deep in furze. It was dark, with a high wind, and a tremendous roaring sea. I could not hear, nor see many yards about me. In this dismal solitude I was suddenly startled by hearing, close to me, a rustling among the furze. It was a great dragoon. I did not know they had any duty there. Supposing him an enemy, and that the French had landed, I challenged him with "Who comes there?" putting myself in a posture of defence. He answered me in a foreign tongue, and stood over me with his sword. I stood with my musket and bayonet pointed at his body, not knowing whether to shoot him or not: perhaps he did not know what to do either. I talked fiercely to him; he did the same to me; but neither of us understood each other. At last he turned his horse about and rode away. After I was relieved I told the sergeant of the affair; he laughed heartily, and said my opponent was one of the German Legion patroles [sic].

About this time I had a providential escape from drowning in the sea. The month of August being warm, we were ordered to bathe in a part of the harbour about two miles from the town of Weymouth. Sea bathing is beautiful to a good swimmer, the salt water being so buoyant. I could swim well, and, with many others, had got out some distance from the shore, in water about seven feet deep, when suddenly, while swimming, I became entangled with monstrous weeds which grew up from

29 Here Jackson refers to the King's German Legion (KGL), raised after the French occupation of the Electorate of Hanover in 1803. Comprised of former Hanoverian soldiers and other continental recruits allied to the British Crown, the KGL's cavalry arm was initially stationed at Weymouth.

the bottom. They were round and strong like so many cords, and ten or twelve feet long. I became bound hand and foot. The more I laboured to extricate myself the firmer I was bound. Being nearly exhausted with struggling, I, with some difficulty, turned upon my back, that I might breathe more freely. I kept quite free from motion. The tide was coming in; and as each wave lifted me up and down, I found to my great joy they had rent my fetters. In this position I let the tide wash me ashore, and resolved to take no more of this kind of pleasure.

In September an alarming occurrence took place, which might have been of the utmost consequence to all England. We had lost the king! His Majesty one fine evening had gone on his usual water excursion, in his yacht, which always returned before dusk; but on this occasion getting out farther than usual, a very thick fog suddenly fell, which baffled the officer who steered the vessel. During the consternation among the town and the military it was thought certain that the French had taken the king, as a French cutter had been seen during the day. However, to the great joy of all, the fog at length dispersed, and about midnight the king was safely landed.[30]

About the middle of October the weather became wet and very cold, and the king returned to Windsor, ordering his Stafford guards to follow him. I have nothing remarkable to note during this march, except a good deal of drunkenness, for which a corresponding amount of punishment followed.

On our arrival at Windsor to take to the castle duties again, the king ordered the facings of our uniform, which were at that time yellow, to be changed to blue, and that henceforth we should be called "The King's Own Staffordshire Militia." This I thought a fine honour to our county.[31]

I was, youngster like, pleased enough with these long marches, that I might see the country and look over the various towns. So it happened in November, in the next year, I was destined to another long march, but of a very unpleasant nature. On the twenty-first of October, 1805, Nelson had captured the French fleet off Trafalgar, and consequently, their crews became prisoners. The "Stafford" was ordered to furnish an escort, or guard, of one hundred men to receive about five hundred of the said prisoners, at a place in Hampshire, on the Portsmouth road, and to march them to a prison called Norman Cross, at Stilton, in Huntingdonshire, a distance,

30 Delays in the HMY *Royal Sovereign* returning to port indeed sparked occasional anxiety, and the whole notion of the King vacationing on the south coast with French invasion imminent gave royal advisers more than a few misgivings. That said, George III was in little real danger of being captured at sea as the royal yacht was obliged to remain inside a robust naval cordon established around Weymouth. See Chedzoy, *Seaside Sovereign*, pp. 71-88.

31 According to Lord Uxbridge's order of 21 May 1805, King George granted this honour to the Staffordshire Militia to convey his 'entire approbation' of the conduct and character of the corps. Blue was the standard facing colour for royal regiments, hence the change from yellow. See Wylly et al, *Historical Records*, p. 15.

probably, of one hundred miles.[32] The roads were horrid bad; the weather – frosty nights and rainy days. The prisoners, poor fellows! with no other clothing than their light and tattered sea dresses, suffered intensely from the cold, especially in the night. After each day's march, they were lodged in large stables, outhouses, and even in pigsties, with sentries over them all night. My young heart, which had never before witnessed such hardships, bled for them. To see them crammed and jammed together in the horse-stalls for warmth, and to hear their pitiful lamentations, was truly heart-rending. In my turn of duty each time I shewed them all the kindness I could, and gave them all I could spare of my food and money. Their food was always soup, provided by a French commissary. Oh, how different was I treated to them, when, in the chances of war, I became wounded and a prisoner, as I shall hereafter relate. To see them turned out in the morning for the march, lame in the feet, and shivering with cold – one half of them shoeless – the muddy roads ankle deep, beat up by so many feet, was a sight truly appalling. The escort was at that time commanded by a young nobleman of Staffordshire (Lord Lewisham), who was major in the regiment, and in this instance his lordship's kind-hearted humanity was commensurate with his noble title.[33] His lordship had compassion on the suffering captives, and seemed to commiserate their lot. As his lordship spoke kindly to them in their own language, the prisoners looked up to him as their benefactor and friend, and would at the morning turn-out, gather about his lordship and tell him their woes. At one of the towns we entered, his lordship bought up a large quantity of shoes, and had them carried in his baggage cart, to supply the poor fellows as they became barefoot and his lordship would, to have some shoes handy carry a couple of pairs in his over coat pockets, as he rode on the march, in case one should become shoeless by the way. His lordship would also sometimes order them a lunch of bread by the way. At length we arrived at the prison, and heartily glad I was to quit this painful duty, and scene of so great a mass of misery and wretchedness.

The above named nobleman could never witness flogging without being much affected; and if he happened to have the command, and the culprit cried for mercy, he would be sure to obtain it.

Soon after my return from this march I received the first grade of promotion, that of a corporal; and in six months afterwards, that of sergeant; so that now, in my twentieth year, I found myself girt about with sash and sword, to the no

32 The world's first purpose-built prisoner-of-war camp, Norman Cross prison on the Great North Road near Peterborough was built in 1796-7. It held an average of approximately 5,500 prisoners at any given time during the Napoleonic Wars. For a detailed study of the camp, see T.J. Walker, *The Depot for Prisoners of War at Norman Cross, Huntingdonshire: 1796 to 1816* (London: Constable & Co., 1913).

33 William Legge, Viscount Lewisham (1784-1853) became 4th Earl of Dartmouth in 1810. Appointed major in the Staffordshire Militia in 1805, he was made colonel in 1812 after Lord Uxbridge's death. For his biography, see *History of Parliament Online* and *The Gentleman's Magazine and Historical Review*, February 1854, pp. 189-90.

small envy of many of my elders.[34] Now as there were separate rooms for the sergeants' dwelling, I rejoiced at having been withdrawn from the ruffian society in the company's barrack-room, which I had endured for three years: I could now silence them who dared offend again with their unrestrained vulgarity. Nor did I use the authority this little rank gave me in any vengeful or tyrannical manner, but adopted such a mode of doing my duty, as to make the men respect as well as obey me. I now found, among my new rank, more agreeable society, which made my life more happy. I found among the sergeants some intelligent men, of good morals, with whom I desired to associate. A Freemasons' Lodge had been established in the regiment, composed chiefly by the sergeants, but attended by respectable town's people also.[35] Always curious, I had an itching desire to know something of the mysteries of this ancient fraternity; I offered myself, and was accepted, and was regularly made in due form, in all the solemn rites and ceremonies, as pertaining to that most noble of all Orders. It being universal, its merits are well known to the world, but its internal workings will ever remain a secret to all but the initiated. The entrance, and after requisites, were very costly to me, but I was highly gratified; I passed through the several degrees which qualified me to receive a Grand Lodge Certificate from London. I delighted to attend the lectures, which were always edifying, instructive, and tending to goodness.

The regiment continued its unremitting drill and field exercises; the young men had grown up tall, and formed a fine front rank, perhaps not to be surpassed in the army. The king, more and more attached to us, would every year review the corps, and give us praise. This good natured monarch was so kindly condescending that in passing a sentinel, who presented arms to him, [he] would take off his hat to him, and perhaps ask him how old he was, where he came from, what trade he was, &c. The king was not only good natured and affable, but good humoured, witty, and loved a good joke; he often walked out, attended only by one of his lords. It may not be amiss to relate an anecdote of him. The king had a large farm, about a mile from the castle, in which he took delight to breed and feed stock, and this got him the technical name of "Farmer George". As he was one day walking, on the way to his farm he met a boy driving some sheep: the king knew them to be his own by the mark upon them. The king, who always talked in a hurried manner, said to the boy, "Hey, hey, boy; where are you going with those sheep?" The boy, who was from Wiltshire, and spoke the broad dialect of that county, said, "I be gwain to tak um to Windsor, zur." "And whose sheep are they?" said the king. The boy said, "I believe, zur, they be Varmer Jarges." "Hey! hey!" said the king: "Farmer George's! Who is Farmer George?" "I dwon't know," says the boy; "but they zay he

34 Jackson was appointed corporal on 7 May 1807, later than is implied here. He was appointed sergeant on 25 January 1808. See TNA, WO 13/1953, 1954, 1807 and 1808 Staffordshire Militia Pay Lists.

35 A footnote in the original text clarifies the lodge number: 'No. 209, Ancient: Earl Moira, Grand Master.' Lodge 209 remains active in Windsor and Eton today.

be the king." "Hey! the king! hey!" said His Majesty. "Did you never see the king?" "No, zur," said the boy, "but I should like to zee un." The king was so pleased with the artless simplicity of the boy, that he gave him a guinea, and said, "Now, boy, you may tell your friends you have seen the king." This was a fact.

Another instance of this good king's jocularity and kind-heartedness, I may relate with equal vivacity. As one day His Majesty was out with a hunting party, eight or ten miles from Windsor, a tremendous storm of rain came on, when all the party took to their heels for shelter where they could. The king, who always liked to give his attendants the slip, if he could, to laugh at them, took his way down a long narrow lane, where he saw a cottage. A woman opened the door, and the king (unknown to her) asked her if he could have his horse put to shelter till the shower was over; she said they had a shed in the back ground, but her husband was out at work, and she was roasting a goose, which she could not leave, as it would burn; but if he would come in and turn the goose, she would herself take the horse to the shelter. The king readily complied with the request, and found the honoured goose dangling by a string before the fire. Before the woman returned the king had with his pencil, wrote a note, inclosing two guineas, saying "To buy a jack," and placed it under a candlestick on the chimney-piece. So the storm ended, the goose well roasted, the king, well pleased with the joke, retired, still unknown to the woman, who afterwards told the story.[36]

In this year (1805) the Staffordshire regiment was ordered to march for Portsmouth, a movement which very much pleased me, affording, as it did, an opportunity of seeing another district of country, and especially so great a seaport.[37] This change was made to relieve a regiment of regulars, ordered for foreign service. The duty here was very hard, having but one or two nights in bed while off duty; and on the clear days we were well worked upon the Downs at brigading.[38] The chief duties lay in the immense dockyard with which I was always gratified, at seeing the wonderful men-of-war building or repairing, some of them seventy and eighty gun ships, on the stocks. I used to climb up into them at daybreak in the morning, before any of the workmen were come, and indulge my curiosity by searching through their innumerable compartments – deck, below deck – with wonder and amazement, until I lost myself. Again, to see the wonderful saw-mills for cutting timber; the astonishing anchor smithy, forging anchors perhaps five

36 Although their veracity is unclear, these stock anecdotes of George III help explain the monarch's personal popularity late in his reign, when Britons lionized their king as a kind-hearted and fatherly figure. The story of the goose and the roasting jack has obvious parallels with the famous legend of the peasant woman who sheltered Alfred the Great when he was fleeing from the Vikings. Unaware of his true identity, she scolded King Alfred after he accidently allowed her wheat cakes to burn through inattentiveness.

37 The Staffordshire Militia left Windsor for Portsmouth on 15 July 1805. See *London Courier and Evening Gazette*, 13 July 1805, p. 3, column 1.

38 The South Downs are a range of gently rolling chalk hills in Hampshire and Sussex.

tons weight; the making [of] the immense cables, measuring more than two feet round; the clanking of the chain gangs of convicts in doing their heavy drudgery; altogether, I thought myself well paid for the march to this place. But this was a very wicked place, and many of our men got punished through its corruptions. We remained here about six months, and then returned to Windsor.

Some short time after this, I had to retrace my steps to Portsmouth on a very unpleasant duty; somehow or other I was often selected for some hazardous and trying job. In this case it was to escort two deserters, of most desperate character, to the Isle of Wight, to be sent to a condemned regiment on some foreign station, never to return home. These two desperadoes had received their sentence in Yorkshire, and, by various escorts, were being brought onwards. They had, by their audacious craft, overcome several parties, and escaped from several gaols, but had been recaptured. Their character was given to me, in writing, as a warning to beware. The adjutant, also, gave me his charge; so that I knew, if I lost them, what would be the consequence to me. However, it happened that I had been once before on a similar duty when a private, so that I was not altogether ignorant of it. I had six men given to form my escort. I handcuffed the two prisoners together, and placed them between my six men, at the same time ordering the men to prime and load with ball, before their faces, and then set off. I resolved, for my own safety, to allow them no indulgence. In marching over Windsor Forest and Bagshot Heath, which were many miles long, the weather – bitter winter, with cutting wind, and sleet, and snow, all the way – had frozen the irons to the prisoners' wrists; towards the end of the day, and approaching a roadside inn, they prayed me to let them go in to warm their frozen hands: humanity prevailed, and, as they had not behaved amiss, I took them in; they then begged to be unlocked for a while, but, oh, no, that would not do for me: people in the house begged for them, but "No" was the answer. The prisoners wanted drink; they had plenty of money. I let them have what I thought proper. They wanted to give me and the men what I liked; this I refused. The company in the house pitied the prisoners, and spoke against "my cruelty," as they called it. The prisoners, encouraged by this, became rude and, had I not been firm to keep on their irons, I might, for my kindness, have lost my two ruffians the first day, as the people in the house were ready to aid their escape. I ordered them out, and threatened them death if they offered to run away. When I arrived in the next town, I found there was no prison that I could trust them in. I obtained a billet for my whole party at a large inn, where there were plenty of soldiers' rooms over the stabling, so that I kept sentries over them all night, still keeping them handcuffed, as I did all the way after, for five nights and days. I was compelled to keep them under this severe restraint. At length, having arrived within the gates of Portsmouth, they begged of me to let them have some refreshment, to which I made no objection, knowing they were then pretty safe so far. While my back was turned, they told my men that I was a young one, but they had never before met with such a one to hold fast; but that I should not, after all, get them over the water to the Isle of Wight, for they would leap overboard and perish first. One of the men whispered this in my ear. However, I went down to the beach and hired a passage boat, with two watermen; the weather was very rough and the run over to Cowes, about an hour. Now, whether or not, to make sure, and not lose them at last, I ordered the two prisoners to sit on the bottom of the boat, and two of my men over them on the cross spar with the butt end of their firelocks over them, ready to knock them down if they dared to stir; so that they saw every attempt was useless, even the most desperate, to escape. I got on shore, marched them up to the depôt at Newport, got a receipt for their bodies, received their curse, and bid them goodbye with gladness. When I returned to Windsor, and produced my receipt, it gave great satisfaction to the adjutant. He questioned me as to their behaviour; he said I had done well to keep them. Yes, but if I had lost them, I knew what he would have done.[39]

I had now to proceed with the same round of duties and discipline as usual at Windsor, with no further movement that year. But in the next (1806) another route awaited me to go over a fresh district of country, agreeable enough for that matter, but a most miserable job it was, which nearly got me into disgrace, though innocent of crime. About this time the Government began to draught the militias, with bounties, into the line.[40] An order came to the Stafford for that purpose, and about three hundred of the men volunteered their services. These draughts continued about every two years after during the war, and [the militia] still filled up again, either by the county ballot or by beat of drum. These men were now to be conducted from Windsor to Winchester, the appointed depôt; thence to be distributed to the several regiments they had chosen. These needed no escort, unless it was to hold them up when drunk on the road. However, six sergeants were ordered to accompany and guide them. Under the command of a captain, I was appointed to go and pay them daily on their march: but, oh! what a scene was this, for five days together. The men had all got half their bounties in their pockets; now every man drunk, every day – every night; all command was lost; such a sight, perhaps, was never seen; three hundred soldiers, mostly mad drunk! They would march how they liked, and when they liked, and here and there stop and fight a battle on the road. They could not be got together in the mornings to march. The captain, being a stern duty man, was deeply vexed at waiting so long in the street every day; could only vent his rage on me, but the real fault, if any, lay in the other sergeants, for they were

39 Jackson would presumably have lost his sergeant's stripes had the prisoners escaped.

40 Desperate to maintain the regular army's strength for overseas campaigns, the British government encouraged militiamen to volunteer into line regiments. Though a decidedly unsustainable solution, given that such transfers drained manpower from the militia, volunteering helped the government avoid instituting conscription for the regular army and provided line regiments with a ready supply of trained reinforcements to replace losses suffered abroad. More than 94,000 men volunteered from the militia between 1807 and 1814 compared with just over 100,000 men who joined the regular army through ordinary recruitment methods. For a fuller discussion of militia transfers see Kevin Linch, *Britain and Wellington's Army: Recruitment, Society and Tradition, 1807-15* (Basingstoke: Palgrave Macmillan, 2011).

all drunk, too, but kept it out of his sight, and I, unwilling to report them, had all the blame to bear. In the presence of the men the captain threatened me that, when he returned to Windsor, he would have me broke, or reduced to the ranks: poor comfort for me, I thought, for all my pains and soberness, for I believe he and I were the only two that were sober all the way. However, having arrived at Winchester, these sturdy Bacchanalians suddenly (and I knew not why) surrounded the captain, and prayed him not to report me at head quarters, as was in no fault; and they made him promise, upon his honour, that he would not. He did so promise. After this they all swarmed around me, and told me of it, swearing, at the same time, if he had not promised to forgive me, he should have had some broken bones to go back with; so they all cordially shook me by the hand, and bid me farewell. We returned; I heard no more of *my crime*, and thus got out of this unmerited scrape.

I had not forgot to communicate with my parents, and still found them embarrassed for the want of trade. It grieved me that I could not relieve them as I would do. A younger brother had gone into the marines, through want of work; and in about two years time returned home again, badly wounded in the head.

The militias had now become a nursery for the army; we, still at Windsor, had always plenty of work at drilling and training new recruits, to fill up our ranks again. This Staffordshire regiment was composed of mechanics of almost all trades, as well as agricultural and horticultural labourers. The king, ever attached to it, was always desirous of employing such of them as suited his purpose, either about the castle, his grounds, or gardens, and in which employ the men never failed to give him satisfaction.

About this time a grand installation of the Most Noble Order of Knights of the Garter, and others, was to take place. The Stafford was sent out of town for a week, the Guards being the household troops, they must be there on that occasional duty. And now, as great and noble things were to be performed above stairs, it was, of course, necessary that a work commensurate should be carried on in the kitchen; so, for the said purpose, twenty-four active young men were selected from the Stafford, and left behind to drudge in the scullery, or do such other work as the master cooks should set them to do. Of the two men who were of my company we have a ludicrous anecdote. The cook that had these two, being over busy, set them to attend a fine piece of beef which he was roasting; all went on well till it was nearly done, when, lo! through their clumsiness, down fell the spit and beef together into the ashes; frightened, indeed, they were, but hastily got it up, unseen, and with a cloth cleaned it as well as they could, and put it down to roast again. Dinner being called, the cook sent up this piece of beef; meanwhile the two men stood quaking with fear. The king, it was said, was very partial to roast beef, and His Majesty partook of this very piece; and after eating of it, sent his equerry down to the kitchen to know who had cooked that piece of beef.[41] My two men, hearing

41 An equerry is a personal attendant to the sovereign, analogous to an aide-de-camp.

the inquiry, stood petrified with fear, and speechless, lest they should be sent away in disgrace. The cook, thinking all was not right, and to screen himself, confessed he had been over busy, and had intrusted it in the charge of two of the Stafford. This answer was returned to the king, when His Majesty, with his good humoured jocularity, said, "Hey! two of the Stafford, hey! O, they can do any thing well; it was well done, well done; tell the cook to let them roast another piece to-morrow." Here, then, was joy unbounded both for cook and soldiers.

Having just now mentioned, but casually, a word about the noble Orders of knighthood, which so honour and dignify our nation, I am reminded that, while at Windsor, I once saw, with high gratification, a procession of The Most Noble Order of the Garter, merely as they passed by me in the quadrangle of the castle, from one apartment to another, in all their magnificent and splendid costume, such as could not be surpassed. It was composed of princes, dukes, marquesses, and earls; none of lower title are admitted into this order. This was, perhaps, not at a time of installation, or the militia could not have been allowed there; the sight was most imposingly grand; I think it was about the year 1805. From this gratifying remembrance, it may not be uninteresting to give some few particulars of our ancient and noble institutions, which have since then come to my knowledge. The Most Noble Order of the Garter is the supreme of all other Orders. It was instituted by Edward the Third, in 1347.[42] Their insignia and habit is the garter, of dark blue velvet, inscribed with the motto, "*Honi soit qui mal y pense*," in letters of gold – in English, "Evil be to him who evil thinks;"[43] the mantle of blue velvet; the hood and surcoat of crimson velvet; the hat of black velvet; the broad collar of gold; and (if I remember right) the lower costume was of white silk; the figure of St. George suspended from a broad dark blue riband; the star, on the left breast, of silver. The number of knights is restricted to twenty-five, exclusive of the sovereign, princes of the blood royal, and foreign princes.[44] Then follow The Most Ancient and Most Noble Order of the Thistle, which is said to have been instituted by King Achaius of Scotland, in 819, but its origin is ascribed to James the Fifth, in 1534.[45] The badges are the star of silver, inscribed with the motto, "*Nemo me impune lacessit*;"

42 The precise year of the Order's foundation is a matter of some debate but 1348 is the most commonly accepted date.

43 *Honi soit qui mal y pense*, the Old French motto of the Order of the Garter, the United Kingdom's most prestigious chivalric order, can also be translated as 'Shame be to him who thinks ill of it'. Several theories have been proposed to explain the origin of this maxim. The most popular version holds that the motto commemorates an incident at a ball in Calais when one of Joan of Kent's garters fell to the floor. As bystanders sniggered, King Edward III picked up the garter and tied it around his own leg, decrying his courtiers' lack of chivalry with this famous phrase.

44 Membership of the Order of the Garter is in fact limited to twenty-four Companions, excluding members of the Royal Family and foreign monarchs.

45 Scotland's highest chivalric order, the Order of the Thistle is second only in precedence to that of the Garter. James II (James VII in Scotland) founded the modern Order in 1687, though it was revived by Queen Anne in 1703. The Latin motto can be translated as 'No one harms me with impunity'.

the jewel, of the figure of St. Andrew, suspended from a green riband, and the collar of gold. This Order is also headed by the sovereign, and composed of noble rank, from the prince down to the viscount. The next is The Most Illustrious Order of St. Patrick, instituted by George the Third, in 1783. It consists of the sovereign, grand master, and twenty-two knights. Their insignia is the star, inscribed with the motto, "*Quis separabit*;" the collar of gold, and the jewel suspended from a light blue riband. The lowest rank in this Order is an earl.[46] Then follows The Most Honourable Military Order of the Bath, established in 1399. It was revived by George the First, in 1725, and remodelled in 1815. It comprises three classes. 1st, Knights Grand Cross, of whom the number is limited to twenty-two,[47] exclusive of the sovereign and princes of the royal blood. 2nd, Knights Commanders, the number of whom is restricted to one hundred and eighty, exclusive of foreign officers holding British commissions. 3rd, Companions, of whom the number is unlimited. The insignia are the star, inscribed with the motto, "*Tria juncta in uno*;"[48] the collar and the badge, suspended from a red riband. This Order is headed by the sovereign, and composed of kings, princes (some foreign), and all ranks and titles down to the baronet, being mostly of high military rank. The second class in this order, Knights Commanders, is composed of admirals and general officers, having commands. This description of my beholdings during my long sojourn at Windsor, may appear to the grave reader tiresome or nauseating, such having simply been the attractive allurements of a youthful novice, who had not been from home; but having an eye to my progeny, for whom I write, the description may be as interesting to them as they were to me.

Now as things went on in a similar round, as regarded myself, for several years, I shall pass on to the year 1809, when our good and gracious king, George the Third, entered the fiftieth year of his reign. On that occasion a most magnificent Jubilee was held at Windsor, but, alas! our poor king was shut up in his castle unconscious of it, afflicted with that lamentable of all maladies, derangement of mind, from which he never recovered, though he lived ten years after.[49] The Jubilee

46 Membership in the Order of Saint Patrick, which became dormant following the creation of the Irish Free State in 1922, was limited to the monarch and fifteen knights under George III, although it was formally expanded to twenty-two knights in 1833, the figure given by Jackson. The motto translates as 'Who will separate [us]?'

47 The number of Knights Grand Cross was in fact limited to seventy-two as per the 1815 reforms, not twenty-two as Jackson states here.

48 The Latin motto translates as 'Three joined in one', a reference to the badge of three crowns, representing England, Scotland and Ireland, worn by members of the Order of the Bath.

49 George III was indeed unable to attend the Jubilee fête at Frogmore due to his failing health and increasing blindness. Instead, his portrait was exhibited in the illuminated temple constructed for the occasion. See Jeremy Black, *George III: America's Last King* (New Haven: Yale, 2006), p. 406. Although George III's illness was long thought to be porphyria, a rare hereditary condition, recent research has challenged this diagnosis, suggesting instead that the king suffered four episodes of recurrent mania as well as possible chronic mania from 1810. See T.J. Peters and A. Beveridge, 'The madness of King George

'North Front of Windsor Castle'. Print from W.H. Pyne, *The History of the Royal Residences*, Vol. I. (London: Dry, 1819)

was celebrated in the town in the most affectionate manner, but in the castle all was solemn silence. The royal gardens at Frogmore, a little distance from the town of Windsor, were made the scene of royal and noble festivity. I, being of the guard on that occasion had the opportunity of witnessing such a mass of splendid grandeur as, perhaps, was never before witnessed in England. To describe it fully I am unable; a few of its beauties may suffice. A magnificent illuminated temple was erected on a lofty mound, at a short distance from the palace, where all the royalty were assembled, and so brilliant and dazzling was its appearance, as to seem built with fire. This was occupied by the king's choir, singing pieces appropriate to the occasion. The temple was approached by about twenty wide steps, widening as they descended to the base of the mound; the choir, in long white robes, singing an anthem, came out at opposite doors, in single rank, moving slowly down each side of the steps, then stood one above another to finish the piece. The solemn manner in which they performed, together with the blaze of light in which they stood, was to me an overwhelming scene of grandeur. Another grand erection, situate[d] in a dark place, in the shape of a noble mansion, started into an effulgent appearance, as though by magic, and had the brilliance of lightning, showing minutely every part of its spacious front, and in a few minutes, again, as though by magic, as

III: a psychiatric reassessment', *History of Psychiatry*, vol. 21 (2010), pp. 20-37. The monarch's deteriorating mental health prompted Parliament to pass the Regency Act of 1811, authorizing his son and heir apparent, the future George IV, to act as Prince Regent on his behalf.

suddenly disappeared. The trees and bushes of the garden were one blaze of light, from variegated lamps. Two hundred rockets were sent up at one time. Britannia, with her trident and Neptune, with his Tritons, and Amphitrite,[50] with her train, were represented, sailing in their watery cars, on the garden canal, the very water of which was made to blaze with water-rockets. The public were not admitted here, except a select few, and those by ticket. Altogether, it was a novelty of the highest order. Meanwhile the regiment was feasted on roast beef and plum pudding; each man his quart of brown stout, at royal cost. The noble barracks were illuminated at night, and dancing and jollity terminated this memorable day of magnificence.[51]

I have drawn out my militia narrative rather longer than I at first intended, and it may be thought a selfish complacency in eulogising and holding up to renown this king-honoured corps, whose merits, as a militia, I have spoken of with a provincial pride; and justly so, as it was an honour to the county producing it. But my intention has not been so much to eulogize, as to show the nature of the discipline required, and duties to be performed, in the general purposes of militia services; as well as to detail the pleasing or painful incidents, as they occurred, relating to myself; and how a young man, entering such a corps, may, if he be so minded, either improve or debase himself; but if he chooses the right path, that is, a right line of conduct, and has intelligence of mind (setting aside the casualties scattered in the way of military life), he may find much pleasure, and profit, from the variety and changeableness of scene afforded him in the round of his duties, which may lead him over various districts of his country; and, mingling with the inhabitants of different counties, he may gather and acquire such knowledge as he, perhaps, would never have obtained, and upon the whole make it a school for the acquirement of information. So, then, he may, if content, sing a line or two of the old corporal's song –

> "Now I find a soldier's life, if taken smooth and rough,
> A very merry, hey down derry, sort of life enough."[52]

In the year 1810, it seemed as though my propitious stars had run their course, and those of malignant influence only were prevailing. Ominous of some mischievous result, I became very uneasy. Our good old adjutant died,[53] and, as though to honour

50 Amphitrite: a sea goddess, the wife of Poseidon (Neptune).

51 For a detailed contemporary description of the Jubilee festivities at Frogmore, see *An Account of the Celebration of the Jubilee, on the 25th October, 1809* (Birmingham: R. Jabet, [1809]), pp. 18-20.

52 This song appeared in the 1807 comic opera *Two Faces under a Hood* written by Thomas John Dibdin (1771-1841) with music by William Shield (1748-1829). The lyrics were reprinted in anthologies under several titles, including 'Who'll Serve the King?', 'Soldier's Life' and 'The Merry Soldier'. See for instance *The Literary Panorama, and National Register*, vol. III (London: Taylor, March 1808), pp. 605-6.

53 Adjutant Preston Valancé died on 20 December 1809. See TNA, WO 13/1956, 1809 Staffordshire Militia Pay Lists.

the non-commissioned officers, the lieutenant-colonel (Desborough)[54] raised up one of the sergeants to that gentlemanly office, obtaining for him a commission. This man, who was of a waspish temper, and malicious disposition, had, while my fellow sergeant, taken some offence at me, which it seemed he never forgot; in fact, he became a very tyrant to all those of his former rank; but as for me, I seemed to be a special mark for his rancour.[55] I could do nothing right to please him, either in the field or out; and many times he punished me with extra duties, most undeservedly, so that I began to think he would, some time or other, pick a hole in my coat that would disgrace me. Seeing the dangerous position I stood in, and no probability of the war ending, to disembody the militias, I secretly resolved to extricate myself from the tyrant's grasp, by extending my service into the regular army, the first opportunity that offered. I was very circumspect in all my actions during that year. Our beloved patron, the king, still in his malady, shut up in his castle. I supposed now some jealousy had sprung up in high quarters; the King's Own Stafford were in 1811, ordered from Windsor duties to Chelmsford, where, in the course of that year, I had my desire accomplished: an order for a draught was received.[56] After considering the important step I was about to take, and its probable consequence, I resolved at once to take the chances of war, and made choice of the Second Regiment of Foot Guards, commanded by His Royal Highness the Duke of Cambridge.[57] About twenty young men volunteered out of my company to go with me, and which number entitled me to retain my rank as sergeant. So thus I take leave of this "feather-bed regiment," as it had been facetiously called, and if the reader likes to follow me, I will shew him a regiment that very often had no bed at all. Now I and my twenty men, with many others for the Guards, were marched up to London by an officer, who delivered with me a written character from the colonel, which I afterwards learned was a good one.[58]

54 Lieutenant Colonel Edward Disbrowe (1754-1818) retired from the Staffordshire Militia in 1812 having served in the corps since 1778. A favourite of George III, he was appointed Vice-Chamberlain to Queen Charlotte in 1801 and served as MP for New Windsor from 1806 until his death. See Wylly et al, *Historical Records*, pp. 7, 16, and *History of Parliament Online*.

55 The adjutant despised by Jackson was evidently Thomas Musgrave. Previously a sergeant in the regiment, he was made serjeant-major alongside John Cooper on 25 January 1808. Musgrave was appointed as the corps' second adjutant on 27 April 1809. After Preston Valance's death eight months later, Musgrave served as the regiment's sole adjutant. See TNA, WO 13/1953, 1954, 1956, 1807-1809 Staffordshire Militia Pay Lists.

56 Jackson's chronology is a year in arrears; the King's Own Staffordshire Militia was ordered from Windsor to Chelmsford and Colchester on 21 April 1812. See Wylly et al, *Historical Records*, p. 16.

57 Prince Adolphus Frederick, Duke of Cambridge (1774-1850), seventh son of George III and Queen Charlotte, served as Colonel-in-Chief of the Coldstream Regiment of Foot Guards from September 1805 until his death. See *ODNB*.

58 Thomas Jackson was discharged from the King's Own Staffordshire Militia on 3 May 1812, beginning his service in the Coldstream Guards the following day. See TNA, WO 97/181/59 and WO 13/1958, 1812 Staffordshire Militia Pay Lists.

2

Entrance into the Second Regiment of Foot Guards

Arrived in London, we were, in a day or two, all clothed in the Guards' uniform, and inspected by the Duke of Cambridge. He was highly pleased with the men; all young, and not one of us under five feet nine. As for me, his highness knew me personally, having seen me so frequently on duty at Windsor. He asked me some questions, and told the colonel, who was with him, that he should confirm me a sergeant; that is never to be reduced without his approbation. Well, thought I, this augurs well, so far. I was immediately ordered to take my turns of duty. The sergeant's dress was splendid, the coat nearly covered with lace, and the cap with ornamental gold chain and tassels. These gilded heroes looked upon me, coming from a militia regiment, as a thing unworthy [of] their notice, much less their society. This made me a little uneasy, but I knew I had been too well trained to need any information of them; but, on the contrary, I soon found many of them lamentably deficient in some particulars and which they were glad to ask of me. I could form no agreeable sociality with them; they were mostly of limited education, but mightily puffed in ignorance, assuming the character of the conceited London swell.[1] The adjutant had almost every thing to do with the regiment, except on field-days; he received all reports, and punished all minor offences; likewise granted all indulgences, &c. He quickly had his eye upon me, but not an evil eye, as my plebeian adjutant had. This was a gentleman, and never found fault with me.[2] Before I had been there two months, as though to test me in some particular

1 Swell: a person of wealth or exalted social status, typically someone regarded as fashionable.

2 This was Charles A.F. Bentinck (1792-1864), son of Major General John Charles Bentinck. He had previously served in the Peninsula and was wounded at Barossa. As adjutant, Bentinck accompanied the Coldstream's second battalion to the Low Countries in 1813 and served as Deputy Assistant Adjutant General to the Second Division at Waterloo. See TNA, WO 12/1709, Coldstream Guards 1812 Pay Lists, and WO 65/62, 63, 1812 and 1813 *Army Lists*. See also Bentinck's entry in David and Janet Bromley, *Wellington's Men Remembered* (Barnsley: Pen and Sword, 2012), vol. 1, p. 92 and Bamford, *Triumphs and Disasters*, p. 33.

duties, he selected me to escort three gentlemen, captains in the French army, who had been taken prisoners, and broke their parole of honour to escape to France. Well for me I had been used to the work before. I had a guard of six old soldiers given me. These gentlemen were to be regarded as common deserters. I received them at Tothill Fields prison; I then made the men load with ball, before them, and made them understand it was for them, if they dared offer to escape. My route was for Chatham. At the end of the first day's stage one of them, who spoke English, hoped I would not send them to prison, but let them go to an inn, and I might put a sentry over them, as they had plenty of money, and would reward my kindness and the soldiers too. My reply was, "I have no alternative; to prison you must go." I knew the trick of drugging the guard. However, I begged of the gaoler to be kind to them, as they were unfortunate gentlemen; but, gaoler like, he paid no regard to the voice of humanity, but turned them in amongst a group of ruffians. It was bitter frosty weather, I went for them at seven next morning, when I was sorry in my heart for them; they were frozen. The ruffians had ill used them, and thrust them out from any warmth. They were too ill to march, so I took them to the first inn that I found open, to warm them, and get breakfast, for which indulgence they were very grateful. Thus, for my own safety, I proceeded every day. On arriving at Chatham, I put them on board the convict ship, obtained a receipt from the port admiral, and returned. The adjutant, in anxiety, sent for me, and was well pleased at my conduct. After this I became as much in favour with this adjutant, as I had been out with the other. This gentleman seemed as though he would lavish indulgence on me, in reserving me for particular duties. Several reinforcements from the regiment were ordered for Spain; and each time it was my turn to go, he always ordered me back.[3] Though I could have wished to go, for after hearing the old ones talk of their battles, I thought I should like to go and see for myself the *reality of war.* I was next sent to a recruiting station; first at Salisbury, and then at Chichester. I remained there many weeks; I disliked that service; I was unsuccessful, not having that gift of trickery – that mean artifice which usually qualified the recruiting sergeant. Disdaining it, I applied to be called in, and was much more happy in my London duties. I had here plenty of time to view the wonders of the great city. The British Museum was most attractive to my inquisitive mind. I had, when on duty there, the privilege of going over it as long as I liked. I always found something to wonder and delight me, especially in those schools for the scientific, the fossil rooms. There, to see the skeleton of a human body; the bones of colossal animals; full skeletons of enormous reptiles, fishes, plants, &c., all embedded in solid rock, of various strata, was to me astounding – wonderful. Since then, having read some little of geology, the remembrance of them has become more interesting. Beside this magnificent exhibition, many others of the fine arts, and other

3 The 1st Battalion of the Coldstream Guards sailed to Portugal in 1809 and saw extensive service throughout the Peninsular War.

'Montague House – now the British Museum'. Coloured aquatint after Thomas Hosmer Shepherd, from Rudolph Ackermann's *The Repository of Arts…* (1813). (Wellcome Library, London)

splendid rarities, were, to my uninformed mind, a new world of information. I was now glad I had made choice of the Guards. In this corps, at London, soldiering was a holiday, compared with the perpetual turmoil of drill and field-work which I had left.

However, it was not for me to rest long together in London. In 1812 fresh demands from the militias were required, to reinforce the army. I was ordered to attend the several militia stations – Chatham, Dover, Portsea, Portsmouth, and elsewhere, to induce men to join our regiment. I succeeded in bringing to the Guards some thirty or forty men, many of whom never found their way home again. Some of them, after sober reflection, repented, and said by the way, "Sergeant, you are leading us to the slaughter-house." I laughed them out of it; but perhaps they were about right. I said I disliked the recruiting service; however, another tour of that kind was marked out for me and another young sergeant, rather of a whimsical nature. It was to take a drum and fife, and attend all the wakes, races, and revels, within twenty miles of London. There we had to strut about in best coats, and swaggering, sword in hand, drumming our way through the masses, commingled with gazing clodpoles,[4] gingerbread mechanics, and thimble-rig sharpers.[5] These

4 Clodpole: an awkward, foolish or clumsy person.
5 Thimblerig is a confidence trick also known as a shell game; a sharper is a cheat or swindler.

pranks ended with the summer; we had not been very successful; our standard ran very high, and the "free, able, and willings" very low. This sort of life might be said to be pleasant enough, and one might have sung the old corporal's song; but I was glad the revelry was over. And now I turn to more serious matter[s].

This year (the eventful year 1813) hurried me into a foreign country, the seat of war; but, by the way, I must relate another important event, prior to that, namely, my marriage. I had formed an acquaintance with a respectable young woman, the daughter of a veterinary surgeon; and seeing others married, and doing well, why should not I? We were married.[6] My wife's friends were opposed to the match, and did not look favourably upon me; my calling was too low. We had been married only about one short month, when rugged misfortune doomed us to separation. Now the tables seemed to be turned with me; and, ominous of reverses, the Dutch had revolted, and threw off the French yoke.[7] An application was made to England for assistance, when, suddenly, the whole brigade of Guards, to a man, were swept away from London, on this expedition, for Holland.[8] And what should be, but the King's Own Stafford Militia should, at last, become the London guards, in our stead.[9] Honoured regiment!

The order was given us on Sunday, after divine service, to be ready to march on Monday morning. Sad news to take home to my dear wife. However, she bore it with great fortitude; as for me, I must look for such an occurrence. The separation was, of course, painful. We parted. The battalion formed in the morning in Birdcage Walk,[10] ready for the word, "March!" The men, nerved with a parting glass, gave, as usual, three wild huzzas, and off we set for Greenwich, the place of embarkation.[11]

6 Thomas Jackson married Maria Hall on 25 September 1813 at St Martin-in-the-Fields Church in Westminster, London, now located at the north-east corner of Trafalgar Square.

7 As Napoleon's fortunes flagged, the Netherlands rebelled against French hegemony in favour of the exiled Prince of Orange in November 1813. A British army under Sir Thomas Graham was dispatched to the Low Countries to support the Dutch revolt and destroy the emperor's naval forces at Antwerp. Keeping the region out of French hands in the hopes of deterring a cross-Channel invasion had been a long-standing tenet of British foreign policy. Graham's show of force was also intended to secure Westminster a say in the fate of the Low Countries during post-war peace talks amongst the allied powers. For more on the background to Graham's campaign, see Andrew Bamford, *A Bold and Ambitious Enterprise* (Barnsley: Pen & Sword, 2013).

8 The entire London-based Guards Brigade did not sail for the Low Countries as Jackson implies here. Seven companies of the 2/1st Foot Guards and six companies from the second battalions of the Coldstream and 3rd Foot Guards were dispatched to the Netherlands under Major General George Cooke, although additional companies were also sent out later in the campaign. See Bamford, *Bold and Ambitious Enterprise*, p. 36.

9 As Jackson suggests, the Staffordshire Militia was ordered from Colchester to London on 21 November 1813 to relieve the Foot Guards from duty at St. James's and Kew Palaces. See Wylly et al, *Historical Records*, p. 17.

10 Named for the royal menagerie and aviary once located there, Birdcage Walk is a street in Westminster immediately south of St James's Park.

11 Ensign Thomas Slingsby Duncombe, describing the march from Westminster to Greenwich for embarkation to the Low Countries, noted that 'never were men more drunk than the major part of the

The old weather-beaten, splinter-shattered, bronze-nosed pensioners, came out of their quarters to laugh us good cheer.[12] On this sudden emergency, all the trading vessels on the Thames were pressed, but [were] very unfit things to accommodate troops. Numbers of them, about Greenwich, were very small ones. The one I got into held our two flank companies, and the staff officers: about two hundred altogether. About four in the afternoon our ship, which was called a "Scotch smack,"[13] began to sail down the river, under a very rough wind and snow, so made but little way, and it was eight o'clock, and very dark, before we had reached the mouth of the Thames. The ship was aground, and could go no further; the tide was going out; the sailors were obliged to carry out two small anchors to a distance, one on each side, to prevent the ship from falling over on her side. In the night she stood on dry land. I feared this was only a presage of some worse disaster. The officers were mortified indeed, but must wait the return of the tide, next morning, about nine o'clock, to raise her up again. And surely the next morning's rough winds did bring with them a disaster – but a hair-breadth escape of being fatal to us all. After getting clear of the river, and standing out towards the North Sea for several hours, the sea became so rough as to frequently bury this little, bobbing up-and-down, vessel. One wave had, but by a miracle of Providence, swept twenty of us off the deck; such as could get below did; others held on by the cords, and endured the wash of the waves. I was very ill, and sick, from the motion of the vessel, and stretched on the lowest bottom of the ship, as were many more. The rough wind continued as we stood farther out, and, about twelve or one o'clock, I heard a most tremendous grinding roar under my head, accompanied by an awful crash. Every one started up, alarmed, cured of their sickness by the fright. It was no less than the ship on an unseen rock, below water, and the rudder torn away! Here was an awful situation – the vessel unmanageable, and on a blind rock, in a tremendous rough sea. A wild scream rung through the ship when she struck. All were hurrying upon deck, and the seamen driving them down, or they could do nothing. The captain of the ship cried out, and very properly, "God be merciful unto us!" Hour after hour passed away in this condition. Our distress was seen from the heights about Harwich, but no boats could live to help us in such a sea. The officers consulted the captain and mate, as to what could be done; the captain said, "Nothing," and advised the soldiers to swim for their lives (at least ten miles) to the nearest land; but none dared venture. Now all was hopeless – ship, and life, and all – the water gaining double the force of the pumps. It was getting dusk, about five o'clock, when, by the mercy of God, the wind suddenly changed about to the very opposite; the ship men then said that if, perchance, they could, by the sails, help the wind to work her off the rocks, she might drift back towards Harwich

Coldstreams.' See Bamford, *Triumphs and Disasters*, p. 32.

12 Jackson here refers to the naval in-pensioners living at the Royal Hospital for Seamen at Greenwich.

13 A smack is a small, typically single-masted vessel used for fishing or coastal commerce.

harbour during the night. Providence helped them. In an hour they succeeded; got her off; and, before midnight, she had drifted into the harbour, and we got safe landed. Thus were we all delivered from that imminent peril. I now learned from the sailors that the disaster had happened through the unskilfulness of this "braw" captain,[14] who did not know the course. We were all then put into a barrack in the high fortress of Harwich; and as there was no shipping to be had, we waited for the repair of this smack of "the land o' cakes."[15]

After a fortnight had elapsed, the urgency of the case required our removal. A man-of-war, which had been captured from the enemy, was brought, as near as she could come in safety, to reëmbark us, again to be committed to the frail water. We were now loaded into a great ugly sailing boat, with no deck, like a great old barge – (I think they called it "lugger")[16] – to carry us about twenty miles out to the ship. The sea began to be rough again, and I [began] to fear another disaster; however, after a good drenching from the snow and the waves, we came up with the ship, a fine, majestic, new-built vessel, of seventy guns. It was here an awkward job for soldiers, loaded like pack-horses, with musket in hand, to climb up the ship's side, as high as a house; but there was no other way for us.

I was delighted with the internal view of this great man-of-war, in her full equipment for service. I soon forgot our late troubles, and glad we had escaped another risk in the "smack," which had twice before *smacked* us to the bottom; but in which, if we had proceeded, I should probably never have told this tale. There was no motion felt from the sailing of this man-of-war, no more than sitting in a house. The weather now became more quiet, and we were but a few days and nights going over the north sea. We were put on ship allowance – salt beef, as stringy as old roping; biscuits, as hard as tiles; and grog of about five water.[17] One of the days was pudding day. My mess had nothing to bag it in, so I cut off my shirt sleeve, which made a very good shift.[18] Now, sailing fair one beautiful calm night, not a rippling wave to be seen; the moon at full; when, on the midnight watch, I enjoyed a most enviable sight, such as I thought worth going a hundred miles to witness. Out of all sight of land; the moon silvering over the smooth surface of the ocean around; the strict discipline in the ship; not a word allowed to be spoke, though, perhaps, a hundred men on deck; the seamen going up and down the shroudings; yet not a word; all in deathlike silence, save the shrill tone of the boat-swain's pipe, which seemed to be the mover of all action. The ship in full sail; the wind just enough to fill the sheets; and to sit on the deck, and look up to the astonishing height of the masts, the vast breadth of the enormous sails, one above another;

14 'Braw' is Scottish slang for fine or excellent, used here sarcastically by Jackson.

15 The 'land o' cakes' is Scotland. The phrase refers to Scottish oatcakes, a national food staple.

16 A lugger is a small sailing ship with two or three masts and lugsails, often used for fishing.

17 'Five water' grog refers to the mixing ratio: five parts water to one part rum.

18 A shift is a long, loose-fitting undergarment, although Jackson is using the term here to refer to a make-shift sack fashioned out of his shirtsleeve.

the brilliant glare of the moon falling full upon the new white canvass, and with nothing to disturb the contemplation of the absorbing scene, I looked upon the enchanting picture with transporting delight, and thought it worthy a place in the best drawing-room of old Neptune's palace.

3

Landing in Holland

As we approached the shores of Holland, the weather grew rough.[1] We were to land at Schieveland [sic–Scheveningen], about two miles from the Hague. Our man-of-war could not approach within five or six miles of the place; a whole fleet of small craft was sent off to fetch us; these were called "skuyts," or scoots.[2] They played like so many corked bottles round our huge ship. They were decked, and close, and held about twenty soldiers each; they ran us to shore, and, as far as they could, aground. The surf was so violent, that small boats could not live; so a great many Dutch watermen, booted up to the waist, buffeting through the surge, carried us on their shoulders. This was a novel sight, to see the sturdy Dutchman, with a soldier on his back; the soldier with his knapsack and great coat rolled on his back, with his musket in hand, while the foaming spray played the water-works over them. We now got safe footing on this land of wooden shoes, and were clear again of the treacherous water. I thought of the words of Robinson Crusoe, who said, after his perils at sea, "Give me one square foot of solid land in preference to a thousand acres of sea."[3]

As soon as all were landed, and formed up, it being dark, a troop of Dutch cavalry appeared, with a lighted torch in the hand of each man; they formed on each side the road. On our march, masses of people headed our column, singing their national songs; also "God save the King," in English. This I thought a pleasing reception. Arriving at the Hague, we were conducted to be drawn up in a large square, illuminated; and from there to be billeted, by the burgh-master, or mayor. We were put into every body's house alike, gentle and simple; and guides from the assembled populace shewed us to our quarters. A laughable incident took place between me and my host. He was a gentleman. Another sergeant (an old soldier,

1 The transports carrying the Foot Guards under Major General Cooke's command arrived off Scheveningen on 6 December 1813, where William, the Prince of Orange had himself landed on 30 November. See Bamford, *Bold and Ambitious Enterprise*, p. 53.

2 Schuyts are Dutch flat-bottomed sailboats.

3 It proved impossible to locate this quotation in Daniel Defoe's *Adventures of Robinson Crusoe*.

'Aankomst van koning Willem I te Scheveningen, 1813' (Arrival of King William I at Scheveningen, 1813). Etching by Reinier Vinkeles after Jan Willem Pieneman. (Rijksmuseum)

who had been there before,) and myself were billeted together.[4] Our guide had just shewn us the door, when this old sergeant was called away; I went in, presented my billet to the gentleman; he read it, then turned to me, talking very fast in a language I was ignorant of. I said, "Sir, I don't know what you say, nor any thing about it; this is my quarters." Of course he knew not what I said. However, he continued his "*non comprend*" to me; his lady came into the hall, and listened; at last he frowningly opened the door, put his hand on my shoulder, and pointed to the street. I, in turn, now frowned; at the same time striking the butt of my fusil on the floor, and said, "I don't care what you say; I am quartered here, and here I'll stop," throwing myself upon a seat. They both started back in perplexity, and stood staring at me. At this moment the old sergeant came in; I told him all about it, as he could speak Dutch. He explained to the gentleman; and it turned out he had provided good accommodation for us at an inn, where he wanted to send me. After the explanation, and a good hearty laugh at me, we were ushered into the drawing-room, to drink a bottle of wine.

4 The Coldstream Guards had previously campaigned in the Low Countries in 1793-5 and 1799.

The people at our new quarters lavished their kindness upon us; the company of the inn came round, wishing to converse with us, but I could only understand through my interpreter, the old sergeant. We halted here one day, to get into some order, after ship ruffling. The first day's march from the Hague I saw a troop of Cossacks, camped in a farm yard, but they had no tents, (I should have said bivouacing), although the ground was covered with snow. These desperate fellows were in their hardihood; the most ruffianly looking soldiers I ever saw from any country: fierce as tigers, with their bristly mouths like a fitchet dog;[5] their flesh seemed crusted with dirt; their arms, accoutrements, and clothing, all of one colour – (the ground) – from head to foot, and shining again with grease, especially their trousers. Their little light horses, fierce, too, with shaggy coats, looked as if clothed in wool-hair. The inhabitants every where hated them, because they would not pay; they would go into a house, take what they wanted, and, if asked for pay, they would present a pistol, and so cry quits.[6]

Now, by this time, all the troop-ships, which had been scattered by the boisterous winds, had arrived, and landed the troops, of all arms, at the most convenient points, and were now on the move, by different routes, and in different divisions. Thus was the great war machinery pressing on the heels of the retreating army of the French, wending its way through the country, to the one concentrated point, in front of the city of Antwerp, there to prepare for a desperate siege. The enemy were, as a last grasping effort, rapidly moving to secure themselves in the two, perhaps, strongest fortresses in the world, viz. Antwerp and Bergen-op-Zoom. The route of my regiment lay through Delft, Briel, Helvoetsluys, Williamstadt, and so on.[7] In all these places, as we passed through, I witnessed the marks of French vengeance on the people for their revolt, written on the walls and shutters of the houses, with cannon, round and iron grape shot, as though the Dutch had harassed their rear, and the French had turned about and raked the streets. The inhabitants generally, so far, were very agreeable, but would give us nothing but what we paid for. They were mostly very poor, from the long and grinding oppression of the French, under King Louis Buonaparte.[8] The chief of their food was coffee, brown bread, and potatoes, with boiled vinegar and butter. The lower orders of these people were the most temperate and orderly I ever saw. Although the Hollands gin was about

5 Fitchet dog: a weasel-like mammal better known as a fitch or pole cat.

6 Cossacks were present in the Low Countries as part of an allied Russian army. British eyewitnesses took a dim view of these soldiers, generally portraying them as ill-disciplined looters. See Bamford, *Triumphs and Disasters*, p. 204.

7 The modern Dutch spellings are Brielle, Hellevoetsluis and Willemstad respectively.

8 Louis Bonaparte (1778-1846), younger brother of Napoleon, ruled over the Kingdom of Holland between 1806 and 1810. He proved a surprisingly popular ruler with his adopted subjects but his decision to govern more in the style of an independent monarch than a French puppet eventually caused his brother to reincorporate Holland into the French Empire. Louis was sent into exile in Austria.

ten-pence per quart, they would not drink it;[9] while the rough English soldier, who had, perhaps, enough allowed him in his rations to do him good, would swallow, at one tip, a full quartern;[10] but ask the Dutchman to take a glass, he would shrug up his shoulders in horror, as though he was offered arsenic. The women, though poor, were always remarkably clean and neat in their dress, as, also, in their domestic habits. There was one peculiar custom of the country, observable in the housewife, rather indelicate to the English female eye. Before she sat down to her knitting, or sewing, she would take an earthen pan, holding about a quart, and put into it lighted charcoal; then place it between her feet, under her coats, and so sit to her work. It was also customary in the ladies going to divine service, to have their servants behind them, carrying these lighted fire-pans for the same purpose. Both men and women, of the lower class, wore wooden shoes, stuffed with hay, which they called "clumpers."[11]

As we approached near to our destination, we were not often allowed to be in houses; the company I belonged to, being light troops, was, with others, always being thrown out in advance; and after outposting all day, in fields or lanes, in frost, snow, or rain, far from any town, our night quarters would generally be in barns, outhouses, stables, and such like. I am now come to the point where I promised the reader, if he would follow me, to shew him a regiment that had very often no bed at all; where, when he lies down, he dares not take off so much as his belts, on pain of punishment. With his knapsack for his pillow, a bit of straw to lie upon, and his blanket to enwrap him, he must be content. This was the rule in the Guards; for in case of a midnight turn-out, which must be done, and on the move, in about five minutes, woe be to the man left behind undressed. Thus, for many weeks together, I have been occupied in one kind or another of these turmoiling duties, and never had my clothes off, so that, by being filthy, I had lice.

At a town called Helvoetsluys, our regiment was for the night put into an old filthy barrack, preoccupied[12] by the French, completely gutted and damaged. It was dark; some straw was obtained for the bedding on the floors. The quarter-master luckily got provisions in the town; the camp kettles were now set to work, to quiet the hungry maw. But here a fatal catastrophe had nearly befallen the whole regiment – the water in the barrack well had been poisoned! About ten o'clock we eat our hungry meal, of meat and broth, without perceiving any harm. Five other sergeants and myself went to lie down in a closet, on the ground floor; in about half an hour our bodies began to swell, followed by a nauseating sickness; vomiting ensued, which continued all night. The same was the case with the whole of the men, but happily none proved fatal. All were in a woful [sic] condition to march

9 Hollands gin, or jenever, is a traditional juniper-flavoured liquor originating in the Low Countries.

10 Quatern: a quarter of a pint.

11 Clogs, known as klompen in Dutch.

12 That is to say, previously occupied.

'The halt, c. 1815' depicting the Coldstream Guards. Watercolour by Orlando Norie, 1854. (Anne S.K. Brown Military Collection)

the next day. I cannot mention every incidental casualty which took place during many weeks marching and countermarching, crossing and recrossing enormous rivers, with which the country abounds, but shall make short way to the grand point of concentration.

It was now dreary December, and the light troops still on scouting duty. We arrived early on the morning of Christmas Day, at a little town called Columntout,[13] where I hoped to enjoy the day in rest; but it was not to be so. I was immediately ordered off, with eighteen men, a mile in advance, as an out piquet. We had no food in our havresacks; and the roads were so bad, that the commissary could not keep up with his waggons. But, food or no food, work must be done. My post was in a dismal woody district – only one poor cottage to be seen. I took possession of an old stable therein, for shelter. After posting my sentinels further in advance, and returning, [I] found the men had made a fire with the garden palings,[14] and had discovered a potatoe [sic] bury, which they had opened with their bayonets, and were roasting them. This was wrong, and I was sorry for the poor people; but, as it is said, "necessity has no law," I was glad myself to make my Christmas dinner of a half roasted potatoe. The "case" here, now, I thought mightily "altered:" instead of

13 Kalmthout or Calmthout, a village twelve miles from Antwerp.

14 Palings: pointed wooden stakes used in a fence.

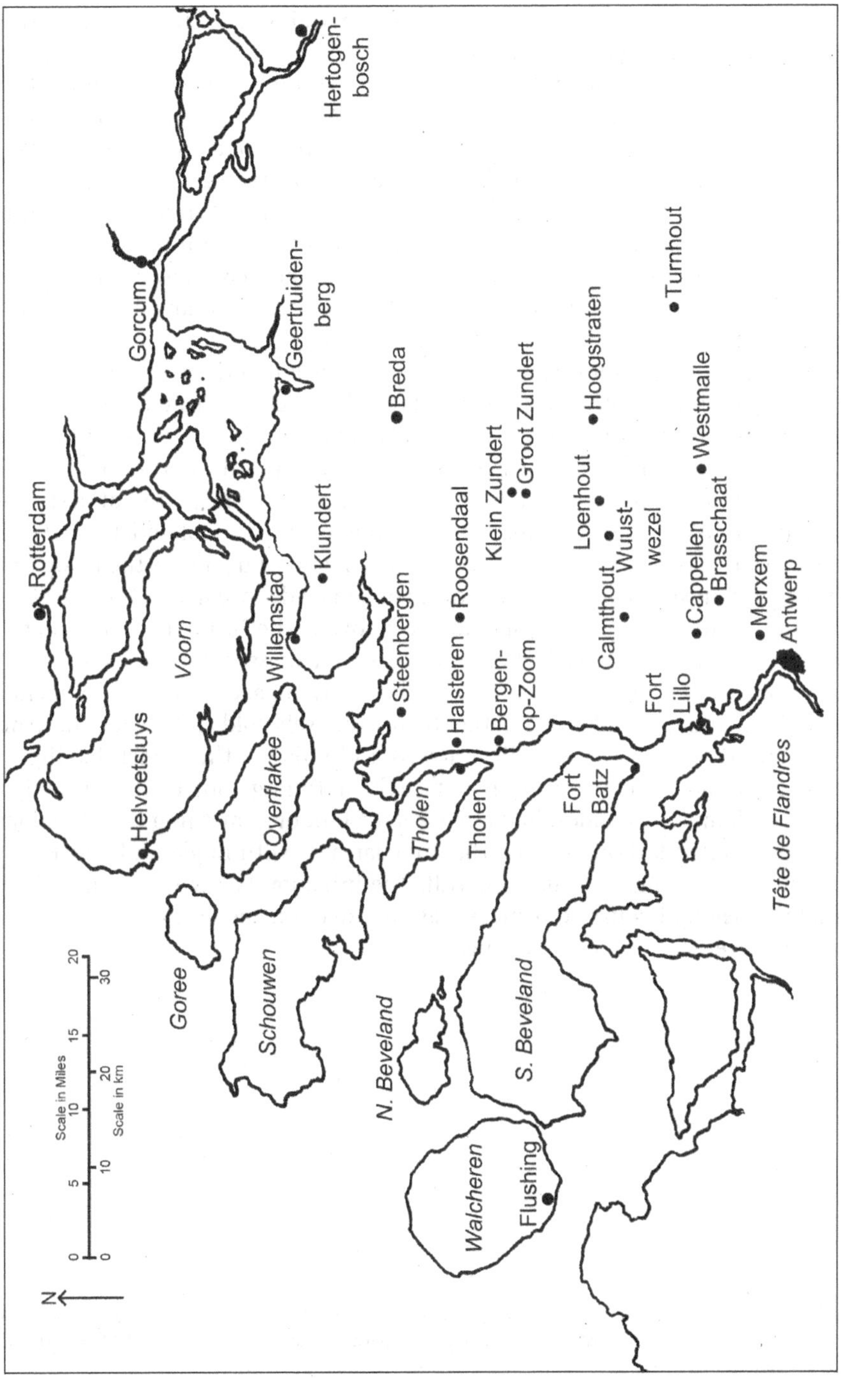

Map 2 The Central Low Countries in 1813.

having our country fare of roast beef and plum pudding, with that humble cheer we passed the day and night, undisturbed.

In the wearisome turmoil of the soldier's life, thus employed, it is never said how he is comforted and fed; how he gets his breakfast, dinner, or supper, or whether he gets any at all. Why, in a country where there are two contending armies, there is every probability of scarcity; or, otherwise, the people are sometimes timid in supplying the one, lest they meet the vengeance of the other, for giving aid to their enemy so that sufficient provision is not always met with in time: in such cases he has it when he can catch it; if he is hungry, he may chew a musket ball; and if thirsty, he may, in Holland, have a nice icicle to cool his angry tongue, and patiently wait for the commissary. This officer is appointed to provide bullocks', or flesh, meat, bread or flour, and spirits, for his division of the army, if he can get it by paying for, but if not, why it must be taken by force. The rule then is, for the quarter-master of each regiment to draw his quota; and the sergeants draw from the quarter-master for the number in each company; and the corporals divide it into messes, and give to each man his mess, or ration, viz. one pound of flesh, one and a half pound of bread, and one-third of a pint of spirits (Hollands), per day. If he (the private) has money, and is in some town, he may buy more. The troops are generally paid, in such cases, once a month; or some advance made. My pay being pretty good, I allowed one half of it to my beloved wife in England; although I knew she could, if friendless, get her living at her business, a dress-maker.

A few more round-about movements, without any engagement, brought us into the month of January, 1814. The weather being intensely cold and severe, the army was cantooned [sic] more in the little towns and villages, the French having no wish to face us, nor had we any desire to face them. In England, it will be found on record, the Thames of London had a market, or fair, or something like it, holden on the ice.[15] Holland, though about the same latitude with England, I considered much colder. Every man's house was full. The inhabitants having no more beds than family need, of course our place was, as usual, on the ground floor: but no undressing, even now, unless to change.

15 Although frost fairs in London were held occasionally throughout the sixteenth, seventeenth and eighteenth centuries, the famous frost fair of February 1814 marks the last time to date that the lower Thames has frozen over.

4

The Siege of Antwerp

Meanwhile, Sir Thomas Graham,[1] the general chief in command, who had been waiting for some heavy ordnance from England, was making preparations for the bombardment of Antwerp; and having got all ready, towards the middle of February, although the weather continued its rigorous severity, the troops of all arms were now put in motion. The light companies of the brigade of guards, after marching about ten miles in the dark and snow, arrived at daybreak, and joined a rifle corps,[2] in advance of the columns, on a plain about two miles in front of Antwerp. Here the French outposts had waylaid us: we could not see them through the snow that was falling. Here a sharp action commenced.[3] The French fell back upon the village of Marksham [Merxem]: there they had every advantage of us, firing from the walls, windows, and doors of the houses; we had no alternative but to charge. The order was given, and with the usual war cry, or wild shout, which always accompanies the English charge, they were chased from their hold, but most imprudently. The men, now too hot to be restrained, run [sic–ran] them within the range of the Antwerp guns, and many were killed in retreating. We found, on the way, the French had put every obstacle in our road: they had cut trenches, six feet deep, across the main road to Antwerp; and felled large trees which stood by the road side, and laid them across also, to obstruct the march of our heavy guns and ammunition waggons. This caused some delay, and some hard work for the pioneers to remove the obstruction. This simple affray caused many a poor fellow, on both sides, to tinge the snow with his blood. The heavy battering trains were with great difficulty got along the snow and muddy roads, it

1 Sir Thomas Graham, (1748-1843), 1st Baron Lynedoch from May 1814, led the 1813-14 British expedition to the Low Countries following distinguished service as Wellington's de facto second-in-command in the Peninsula. See *ODNB*.

2 Four companies of the 95th, drawn from all three battalions of the regiment, served with Graham's army in the Low Countries.

3 The engagement described here is the Second Battle of Merxem, fought northeast of Antwerp on 2 February 1814, not 'towards the middle' of the month as Jackson implies. For more on this action, see Bamford, *Bold and Ambitious Enterprise*, pp. 129-141.

taking ten or more horses to draw one of them, either gun or mortar. Now having taken up the right position, whole regiments were ordered on fatigues in the night, under the direction of the engineers, to build batteries for the guns and mortars. It was surprising to see the quantity of earth dug up, and raised into a rampart, in one night: the excavation left a trench as wide, but deeper than a canal, stretching across a field. The battery position was near to the village of Marksham [sic – Merxem] – about a mile distant, on the great road to Antwerp. It was thought all our forces and power was not half sufficient to attempt the reduction of this great, impregnable city. But the gallant hero of Barosa,[4] whose characteristic was death or victory, was not to be restrained, neither by the frigid elements, nor the lack of force, but trusted to his own skill in command, and the undaunted intrepidity of his troops; disregarding the enemy's strong position, or their superior numbers, he would "have at them."

I heard that the Prince of Orange had requested General Graham to spare the city for the inhabitants' sake; so that he turned the bombardment principally to the destroying of a large fleet of men-of-war, belonging to France, lying in the grand basin of Antwerp; but in this the French had anticipated him, and had them secured, bomb-proof, by a covering of six feet thick of turf upon their decks.[5]

The terrible thundering work at last began, from six eighteen-inch mortars, ranged in one battery, and a number of heavy guns planted in the same line; the mortar shells probably weighing three hundred weight, and the gun shot, thirty-two pounders; the shells being chiefly directed to the shipping, and the cannon shot to the Antwerp batteries.[6] My company was ordered to form a guard, as is usual, at the back of these six mortars. Their astounding and stupifying report, made one leap off the ground; and the tremendous recoil actually forced them through the wood frame work, half over head, although the ground was frozen as hard as stone. We had to stand here several hours. The French soon got our range, and answered us with their shells, which often fell among us in the battery, wounding both the artillery and our men. My position here was extremely perilous. The old corporal's song, I thought, was now quite out of tune. I might rather have said, with the old sailor, in the tempest, "This quite puts my pipe out."

4 Graham prevailed over Marshal Victor at Barrosa on 5 March 1811 as part of an unsuccessful Anglo-Allied effort to lift the French siege of Cádiz during the Peninsular War.

5 The French defenders indeed covered the decks of naval vessels at Antwerp with thick layers of dung and clay to make them as fireproof as possible. See Bamford, *Bold and Ambitious Enterprise*, p. 148.

6 Jackson misrepresents the actual artillery employed during Graham's bombardment of Antwerp (3-5 February 1814). Twelve artillery pieces (four 10-inch mortars, two 8-inch howitzers and six long 24-pounders) shipped from Britain were joined by thirteen mortars, varying between 12 and 7½ inches in calibre, brought up from the garrison of Willemstad. Several of these guns, however, were disabled by French artillery fire, and the available ordnance proved insufficient to the task of reducing Antwerp or destroying the French fleet, causing Graham to abandon the bombardment and retreat on 6 February. See Bamford, *Bold and Ambitious Enterprise*, pp. 142-157 and Appendix V, p. 274.

The French were extremely clever in throwing the shells to a nicety: when I have been marching a column, at a mile distance, they would either drop them into our ranks, or burst them a few yards over our heads. Being relieved from that unwelcome situation, the snow falling fast, we were ordered to go into the houses of the village close by.[7] About twelve men, with me, went into a front house: the men, all hungry, seeing no fire or wood, soon fetched down a door, broke it up, and lighted one. We had raw meat in our havresacks, and every man, with his mess-pan, was employed in boiling his bit. The French, now, as though to spoil our comfortable dinner, must visit us here, too, with a tremendous explosion at the back door: a shell had struck the gable end of a house, broke it in, and down fell the roof. The family, in another room, terrified, clung to me to save them; I opened the door, and pointed out a way for them to fly. They were soon gone. As I stood looking through the front window, another shell fell in the middle of the street; I had just time to take one step aside, when it exploded, and dashed in the window and frame. The men were all lying or sitting on the floor, but no one was hurt. Caring nothing for these French *frolics*, and every one intent on his mess, when lo! an order came to turn-out; every mess-pan was emptied, the parboiled meat returned to the haversack, and the whole of us ordered to the rear, out of range of the shells. At the moment of the explosion of the above shell, two young officers were passing, arm in arm, and became its victims: it took a leg from each of them: and there they lay till some of their regiment found them.[8]

Although we had here harassing days, my company had pretty good quarters a night. These were in a Roman Catholic chapel, with good straw on a stone floor. I could have slept well but for the noisy bursting of the French shells about our ears. Half our regiment had been, a few days before, quartered in a village Protestant church: we had straw in the pews to sleep on. We remained here several days. The cooking kitchens were between the banked up graves. I was sorry to see the sacrilegious rapacity of our soldiery, in tearing up the pews to make fires; but still, there was not enough to be had elsewhere. To return to my Catholic quarters: I was very much delighted, every night, in watching the interchange of bombshells, between our batteries and those of Antwerp – they always kept on till midnight. Oh, it was a grand sight! The shell, in its range, describing a fine rainbow arch, and a rotary motion upon its own axis, shewing beautifully the brilliant hissing fuzee, as it turned over and over. This was all very well, so long as they kept at a distance; but

7 The village Jackson refers to here is Merxem. Packed with British troops, Merxem was regularly targeted by French artillery during the British bombardment of Antwerp.

8 The two officers who lost legs to French artillery fire were Lieutenant Robert Stowers and Ensign George Chapman of the 2/37th Foot. This unfortunate episode was evidently well-publicized in Graham's army, for it is frequently recounted in memoirs of the Netherlands campaign. Some accounts record that a third officer was walking between Stowers and Chapman at the time but escaped without injury. See Bamford, *Bold and Ambitious Enterprise*, pp. 147-8.

what was now giving me pleasure to look upon, was, perhaps, giving pain or death to some poor fellows wherever they had fallen.

Our general continued this kind of sport, unremittingly, six days and nights. I know not now how many men we lost, but it must have been some hundreds.[9] Sir Thomas, seeing he could make no available impression, either on the fleet or the Antwerp batteries, at length raised the siege. The army was worn out with fatigue. Some fires were left burning, and some effigies of soldiers set up in the batteries. We then decamped in the night. It seemed to be my lot to be one of the first in danger, and the last out; for when advancing, my place was always in the front, but now we were running away, I was in the rearguard – the last of all behind. The division in which I was then moving had retreated about seven miles in the snow, when the commander of it saw a very large farmhouse.[10] He sent to demand it for the use of the officers for the night, and the barns and stabling for the men. My company seized upon one stable, and drove out a dozen fat horses and, taking possession of their warm places, got a few hours' sleep. We were now countermarching our way, two or three marches, to a town called Rozendaal, and its environs. Here we were put into every man's house; good quarters, to be sure, but no beds, but the usual brick floor, and "stromell," as the Dutch called it.[11] We remained here in quiet for a fortnight, not guessing at what should come next; but our indefatigable old general – never idle – was, meanwhile, cutting out some desperate work afresh for us, in the bold and daring enterprise of a night attack on the impregnable fortress of Bergen-op-Zoom; a place so strong, both by nature and art, as to bid defiance to all besieging armies, and had not been captured for nearly a hundred years before, and then only by assault and stratagem. Bergen-op-Zoom may be found in history by the name of La Pucelle, or the Maiden Fortress.[12] The river De Zoom, which is a branch of the noble Scheldt, runs through it.

9 The British bombardment of Antwerp actually lasted from 3 to 5 February and casualties were much lighter than Jackson suggests here. Graham's army suffered 153 casualties (killed, wounded and missing) at the Second Battle of Merxem on 2 February and only 60 casualties from 3-6 February. See Bamford, *Bold and Ambitious Enterprise*, Appendix IV, pp. 272-3 quoting TNA, WO 1/199, pp. 581-2, 589.

10 The 2nd Battalion of the Coldstream Guards were part of the Guards Brigade led by Colonel Lord Proby in the First Division of Graham's Army under Major General George Cooke.

11 Strommel: straw or rushes used for floor covering.

12 After withstanding two Spanish sieges during the Eighty Years' War, Bergen-op-Zoom came to be known as the Maiden or Virgin fortress. The fortress was however taken and sacked by a French army in 1747 led by the Comte de Lowendal during the War of Austrian Succession.

5

The Disastrous Attack and Storming of Bergen-op-Zoom

The troops now having been refreshed and comforted were ready for another desperate enterprise. In the first week in March we were on the move, but none but the commanding generals of brigade knew where, or to what destination, or what was to be done. We were marched about in circuitous routes for several days, and often in the night, as though to perplex the enemy as to what we were about, until the night of the eighth of this month. My company, and other light companies, had been at outposting, and scouting all day in the woods and roughs till nine o'clock, p.m. We came up with our own regiment, which was standing in column of sections. The company was ordered to the head of the column, to take the lead as usual.[1] This move excited my suspicion, that some secret rough job was about to be done. We stood at the entrance of a long dark narrow lane; silence was now imposed on every man, on pain of punishment. We had no idea of Bergen-op-Zoom, nor where it was, so curiously had we been led about. The word to march was given in a whisper. There was something in this movement which struck peculiar awe to my mind: the darkness of the lane, the remarkable stillness of the night, the dead silence of the troops, the heavy crash of the military step on the frozen snow and ice, together with the jingling clank of the light guns in the rear, was seriously impressive. The end of this lane brought us into a large farm yard, up to the knees in straw and snow. Here we halted. We were but another field's length from Bergen-op-Zoom. The secret now comes out. We are told in a whisper that we were about to storm the fortress. Every man was now ordered to strip off his knapsack and great coat, and leave them where he then stood. Our twelve pioneers were here ready, each with an escalading ladder. Another move brought us to the bottom of the field. The first obstruction we met, was a deep dry ditch and lofty spiked palings; these the pioneers had to cut a way through with their axes.

1 Jackson was part of the Guards column led by Colonel Lord Proby charged with executing the 'Left Attack' on Bergen-op-Zoom's Bastion 'Oranje'.

It was now about ten o'clock.[2] We got footing on the outer bank of the great ditch which surrounded the town. This was a moment of deep excitement. My company was to mount the rampart first, and we were soon busy in placing the ladders. The French at this point were certainly taken by surprise, or they might have cut us all off while planting the ladders on this side and the one opposite. The ditch was about twelve feet deep down to the ice, and about twenty wide, and walled up each side. It is usual in desperate cases like this to send the juniors first into danger. The officer leading the first section was a junior. I was the junior sergeant. He was an ensign (a young man) and was much frightened.[3] I was not so well pleased myself at having such a job at that time of night. The French began to fire upon us in the ditch and also on the top. I had lost my young officer in the dark, and concluded he was killed, so was obliged to lead the men up to the rampart myself. Luckily, as there were two other points of attack going on at the same moment (perhaps more alarming), the French were suddenly drawn away from this point, and my company got up with little further hurt. Meanwhile a sad disaster had nearly took place among ourselves. As the men came up the ladders, I formed them at about thirty yards distance on the rampart, when a scattering fire commenced upon the men already formed, from an ambush of the French; the men, without any order, instantly turned round and fired upon their comrades, as they came up the ladders, supposing, as the night was dark, they were the enemy. These again returned the fire, supposing their comrades the enemy. It was a wonder that I was not killed by my own men, as I stood between the two fires. I threw myself on the snow and called to them with all my might, shouting, "For God's sake, men, cease firing; you are killing your own comrades." They did not hear for a minute, but at last I stopped them. By this time all the light companies were on the ramparts, also the captain and colonel.[4] Observe, here, that the companies in the Guards are commanded by colonels; they have also a captain, lieutenant, and ensign.[5] The detachments of the First, Second, and Third Guards

2 Bamford estimates that the guardsmen only reached the Bastion 'Oranje' at 23.30, over an hour after the first attackers had gained entry to Bergen-op-Zoom elsewhere, and by which time the other British columns had been repulsed or thrown into disarray. Indeed, the late arrival of Proby's column, partly due to the long march required to reached their objective from their staging area, contributed significantly to the ultimate failure of the British assault. See Bamford, *Bold and Ambitious Enterprise*, pp. 200-202.

3 Probably Ensign Mark Beaufoy (c.1794-1854), commissioned 12 November 1812. See TNA, WO 12/1710, Coldstream Guards 1813 Pay Lists; WO 17/273, Coldstream Guards 1814 Monthly Returns; WO 65/64, 1814 *Army Lists*. See also Beaufoy's entry in David and Janet Bromley, *Wellington's Men Remembered*, vol. 1, p. 28.

4 By 'the captain and the colonel', Jackson is presumably referring to Captain Charles Augustus Shawe and Lieutenant Colonel Robert Mercer. See footnotes 6 and 14 in this chapter.

5 Jackson is referring to the custom of double-ranking, wherein officers of the Guards held army ranks more senior than their regimental ranks. Thus, commanders of Foot Guard companies were addressed as lieutenant-colonels, not captains. This longstanding practice, in recognition of the prestige of these household regiments, was only abolished in 1871.

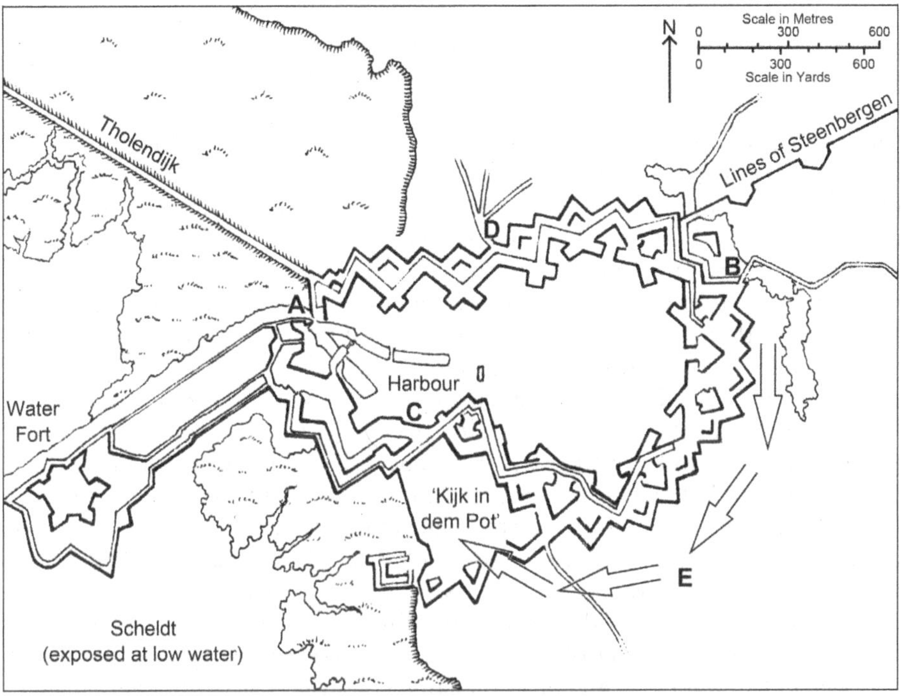

Map 3 The Storming of Bergen-op-Zoom, 8 March 1814.

A Right Attack (500 stormers and 600 supports, under Lt. Col. Carleton) to attack from Tholendijk across the harbour mouth.
B Centre Attack (600 stormers and 600 supports, under Lt. Col. Morrice) to attack across the frozen ditch between the 'De Zoom' Ravelin and the Breda Gate.
C Left Attack (600 stormers and 400 supports, under Colonel Lord Proby) to attack the Bastion 'Oranje'.
D False Attack (650 men under Lt. Col. Ottley) to demonstrate against the Steenbergen Gate.
E Subsequent movement of Centre Attack survivors to join the Left Attack at the Bastion 'Oranje'.

Sergeant Thomas Jackson was part of Proby's Foot Guards column charged with executing the 'Left Attack' on the Bastion 'Oranje'. Following the failure of the assault, Jackson lay wounded in what he described as a 'meadow'; this was almost certainly the Kijk in dem Pot, which had once accommodated an entrenched camp within the city's outer defences.

had next to come up our ladders, in performing which they suffered severely. My gallant colonel, whose name was Mercer, an old soldier, one of the bravest of the brave,[6] now led us over a long range of ramparts into the town, shot at all the way, but from where we could not tell, the French were so securely ambuscaded.

About eleven o'clock most of the columns had worked in at the two points of attack, the one towards the Antwerp gate, and the other to the right of the new gate. The machinery of death was now getting into full play. The roar of cannon and musketry was awfully going on in every part of the town, ramparts, and batteries; some of the columns suffered most severely before they reached the ditch, from the cannon grape shot. The French threw up large blazing rockets, by the light of which they could see where to point their guns. But, wonderful to relate, the desperate intrepidity of the English soldiers – although they had to ascend the ladders, under the guns, and the enemy firing into their very mouths, and if they reached the top they were in the cannon's mouth – yet, despite all these disadvantages, in less than an hour had charged some of the batteries, taken their guns, made about a hundred prisoners, and forced them down the ladders out of the town. Our colonel had led us into the streets, to take our part in the affray. Here we found a mixture of all regiments, charging and firing in all directions, and some of them in great confusion, having lost their officers. We did not at first know them from the enemy, but by the challenge.[7] As all the other regiments wore their great coats, so did the enemy; consequently, some of our street divisions, through the darkness of the night and confusion, mistook each other for the enemy, and fired into one another, as it was almost impossible to hear the challenge, or the watchword in reply.[8] To give an idea of what must have been the carnage in the town during this tragic night, let the inference be drawn from the number of officers and men killed, wounded, and missing, named in the despatches to London afterwards, including the two generals, Brigadier General Gore[9] and Major General Skerrett,[10] whose lamentable memorials are to be seen grouped – if I remember

6 Lieutenant Colonel Robert Mercer of the 2/3rd Foot Guards, a veteran of service in Egypt and the Peninsula, commanded the light infantry companies of the Guards Brigade during the storming of Bergen-op-Zoom and was killed during the assault. Although perhaps an 'old soldier' in terms of battlefield experience, having been commissioned as an ensign in 1799, Mercer was only thirty-one years of age in 1814. For a brief obituary, see *The Gentleman's Magazine*, vol. 84, May 1814, p. 525.

7 The challenge or watchword set for the assault was 'Orange Boven'; see footnote 16.

8 The widespread wearing of greatcoats on account of the cold weather during the 1813-14 Low Countries campaign made it difficult for British, French and Prussian forces to tell friend from foe, resulting in several friendly-fire incidents. See for instance Bamford, *Bold and Ambitious Enterprise*, pp. 99-100, 119.

9 Brigadier General Arthur Gore (1773-1814) was indeed killed at Bergen-op-Zoom. Born in Kilkenny, Ireland, he was commissioned ensign in 1788 and served in India for two decades. Gore fought at Seringapatam and commanded the 33rd Foot for eleven years.

10 Major General John Byne Skerrett (c.1778-1814), mortally wounded at Bergen-op-Zoom, was the son of a lieutenant general. Though certainly a brave officer, Skerrett's blunders in the Peninsula repeatedly

'Springen van Laboratorium Stoelemat te Bergen op Zoom, 1831' (Explosion of the Stoelemat Laboratory at Bergen-op-Zoom, 1831). Anonymous, after Michel Mourot, 1840. (Rijksmuseum)

right – on one pedestal (marble), in St. Paul's Cathedral, London,[11] and all other ranks down to the ensign, which were no less than one hundred and one;[12] the missing are generally somewhere dead and not found. My company had this sort of work for about two hours; we met but few of the French in bodies to fight us fair; they were hidden behind walls, up passages, and in houses, cutting us off in our every movement. Firing from upper windows and roofs of houses, they had every advantage of us.

Our colonel now seeing the ranks of his light companies thinning so fast, and perceiving to keep his ground would be a useless waste of life, withdrew us from the streets to the rear of the buildings, and posted us across a low avenue running parallel with the buildings and the ramparts, under which some large doors opened into, probably, their arsenal; our left standing against the palings of a large garden.

called his judgement into question. See Bamford, *Bold and Ambitious Enterprise*, pp. 64-5. For a contemporary obituary, see *The Gentleman's Magazine*, vol. 84, April 1814, p. 415.

11 The monument to Gore and Skerrett is in the north transept of St. Paul's Cathedral.

12 A footnote in the original text reads as follows: 'I have forgotten the number of men killed, but there were about four thousand engaged.' Jackson is correct; Graham's various assault columns, according to his own dispatch, comprised about 3,950 men. As for casualties, 126 officers (including staff officers) and 2,434 other ranks are listed as killed, wounded or missing in official returns. The total number of British prisoners was calculated as 2,058 all ranks, including 93 officers, 93 sergeants and 1,872 rank and file. For further details, see Bamford, *Bold and Ambitious Enterprise*, p. 182 and Appendix VI, p. 275.

We were here again annoyed by the enemy's fire from the back windows of the house belonging thereto. The colonel then ordered the young ensign – (who had come to life again) – to take twelve men, break the house open, and clear it of the annoyance. A pioneer with his axe soon cut a way through the palings, and also the back door of the house. The men had proceeded about half way up the staircase, when a party of the enemy fired upon them from the landing, and killed and wounded several. One man received a ball in his eye, which passed out near his ear, still he lived! The men then fell back. My young ensign was now very much terrified, and ran to tell the colonel what had happened, but he quickly made him go back. The men now forced their way up stairs again, firing as they went up. They dashed into a large chamber, and bayoneted every one of the enemy: and this house, in the turn of chances, became an annoyance to the French in the front street. My position in this avenue was a most unenviable one – the French seemed determined to dislodge us. They were ambuscaded just in front of us, on the glacis, or outer slope, of the rampart, upon the scarp wall of the ditch. From this situation they threw up a sort of blazing rockets, by the light of which they could see us, and, thereby, take their aim at us, and so kept firing upon us, and we not allowed to fire at them. In this perilous position we stood for about two hours, looking for death every moment; but, yet, after passing through the showers of shot during the night, crossing each other from every point of the compass, I began to think myself invulnerable, and that, by and by, the French would surrender the town to us; and, for a while, was indulging the fallacious hope that I should still escape unhurt. Alas! the moment was near at hand when I should experience the reverse. In the intervening moment another desperate hazard awaited me. The brave and daring colonel (Lord Proby) of the first column of the Guards, had, alone, been reconnoitring the ramparts, and discovered the annoying ambuscade above named;[13] he came down to my company in haste saying "A sergeant here!" I, being near, answered him. He said, "Take a file of men, and go and kill those men on the glacis." I tapped two men on the back, they followed me; poor fellows! there was but one step for them between my tap and their death. I feel the force of the tragedy while I write it. We went boldly up to them, in a quick step, and just far enough to have a slight glance at them, when my two men were dead in an instant. And why not me? I thought after; but by a miraculous interposition of God's providence, as their shots followed me down the rampart to my company. I had not been back many minutes, before my gallant captain (Shaw) was severely wounded: a brave man, that never feared shot nor shell,

13 Colonel John, Lord Proby (1780-1855), styled as 2nd Earl of Carysfort from 1828, was commissioned as an ensign in 1794 and was made lieutenant colonel in the 1st Foot Guards in 1803. Having previously served in Egypt, Sicily, Walcheren and the Peninsula, he commanded the Guards Brigade at Bergen-op-Zoom. Although made a full general in 1846, Proby never again saw active service. Proby served as a Member of Parliament between 1805 and 1807 and again from 1814 to 1818, but his mental health deteriorated, apparently due to fever or injury suffered on the Walcheren expedition, and he never took his seat in the House of Lords. See *History of Parliament Online*.

'Kerk en Markt te Bergen-op-Zoom' (Church and Market of Bergen-op-Zoom). Pen and ink with watercolour by Abraham de Haen, 1739. (Rijksmuseum)

as I had often witnessed.[14] But what had become of my young ensign, I never knew; he, perhaps, was killed in the house before mentioned. Two of the men had carried the captain away to some outside place as I supposed.

The church or cathedral clock now struck four, on the morning of the ninth.[15] The French, still more determined to drive us from our position, had reinforced theirs in their lurking place. They now sallied out upon the broad rampart above us, and, formed in line, shewed a front (by snowlight) of about one hundred men. They advanced slowly towards the slope of the rampart under which we were posted across the avenue. Our colonel in a loud voice demanded, "Who comes there?" Our watchword that night was "King George the Third."[16] The wily French

14 Captain Charles Augustus Shawe (1791-1876) was wounded 'severely' but 'not dangerously' at Bergen-op-Zoom. Shawe had previously served in the 1st Battalion of the Coldstream Guards in the Peninsula from 1810 to 1812; he later received the Military General Service Medal for Busaco, Fuentes d'Onoro and Ciudad Rodrigo. See his entry in David and Janet Bromley, *Wellington's Men Remembered* (Barnsley: Pen and Sword, 2012), vol. 2, p. 265 and *London Gazette*, Issue 16867, 14 March 1814, p. 563.

15 Presumably the clock of the Gertrudiskerk, the church that dominates the centre of Bergen-op-Zoom.

16 The British watchword on the night of the storming was in fact set as 'Orange Boven', or 'Orange on top', a slogan used by supporters of the Dutch House of Orange, with the countersign or reply expected from friendly troops being 'God Save the King'. See Bamford, *Bold and Ambitious Enterprise*, p. 180.

had got hold of it, but could not pronounce it. They answered "Tin Geor de Tir." We were then assured they were the enemy. The soldiers, maddened at standing so long to be shot at, up with their muskets to fire, when the colonel, not availing himself of the first fire, bid the men wait. The French instantly took the advantage, and fired a volley into us at about thirty yards distance. This fire killed my gallant colonel,[17] smashed the bone of my leg in the middle, and killed and wounded many of the company I belonged to, and also many more of the Guards, who had by this time formed in the rear of us in close column. I did not then suppose I had been hit by a ball, but thought it had been from a blow of one of the men's muskets that had fallen. However the leg doubled under me, and let me down. The remainder of the enraged men returned the fire, set off and ran up the rampart without any commander, rushed upon the French, and I never saw them afterwards. While in the hospital I was told, by some of the wounded, that they charged them in full chase through the streets into their barracks, and then fired at them through the windows. Some time after this the two men who carried away the captain returned, and seeing their company gone, kindly asked me if they should carry me away. This is the time that proves the love and respect of the men to their officers, or non-commissioned officers, as too often, in such cases, the tyrant is sacrificed to their hatred and revenge. I had bound up the broken place of my leg as well as I could with my handkerchief. One of the men got me on his back, and the other, holding up my dangling leg very carefully, carried me to the ladders, in the hope of getting me out of the place; but I could not get down the ladder with one leg. I was now in the most excruciating pain. The men said they would carry me any where I liked to go. From the lofty rampart on which we stood, and being mounted, I thought I saw, across a sort of meadow at the lower extremity of the town, a place free from firing, and said, "Take me that way." But, lo! by the time we had reached the middle of the meadow, I found the work of death going on there also.[18] The balls, like a flight of small birds, were whisking thickly past us. I looked for all three to be killed, and said, "You shall carry me no further; it shall not cost you your lives to save mine, so set me down here, and make your escape if you can, till you find your company." With some reluctance they did, and, bidding me farewell, ran off. Here I laid down in the snow, for, indeed, I could not stand, to amuse myself till daylight came, to shew me some better object than that of watching the flashes of the cannon and musketry, and listening to the whiz of their balls.

It was now about five o'clock, and the desperate struggle still going on as fierce as ever; neither side would surrender. Several times during the night, by the desperate bravery of our troops, many of the gun batteries were charged and

17 Lieutenant Colonel Robert Mercer; see footnote 6.

18 The 'meadow' described by Jackson was almost certainly the Kijk in dem Pot, which once accommodated an entrenched camp within city's outer defences. It remains open parkland in modern-day Bergen-op-Zoom.

'The Attack on Bergen-op-Zoom'. From James Grant, *British Battles on Land and Sea*, Vol. II. (London: Cassell, Petter & Galpin, 1873)

taken; and as often retaken, but at great sacrifice of life on both sides. The rattle of musketry was unabated until about nine o'clock, when the ammunition of the English became expended; they were then forced to give way. Confusion now took place; the men running here and there; parts of different regiments, mixed together, came running over this meadow; they halted in a confused mob round about me; they trod upon me, and hurt me very much. The French, in a body, pursued them, and most unmercifully fired into them as they stood defenceless. This fire gave me many more companions in the red and white snow for the day. The remainder of the retreating party ran to the rampart to [the] ladders, thinking to escape thereby; but while they were thus running, the French turned the guns of an opposite rampart and slaughtered them. Many reached the ditch, but found that a depth of water had been let in from the river. Here many were drowned, and many shot, while struggling for the last means of escape in the ditch. The major-general (Cook) who commanded the whole of the English inside the town, seeing it a useless loss of life to continue the contest, surrendered, and we all became prisoners.[19]

19 Major General George Cooke (1768-1837), who had joined the 1st Foot Guards as an ensign in 1784, was a veteran of previous British forays to the Low Countries and had served under Graham at Cadiz. The

About ten o'clock the firing had all ceased, and thus ended the twelve hours' storm, which, perhaps, for its long and obstinate continuance, and sharpness of action, stands unparalleled in the history of the wars. The firing now ceased; the French soldiery were let loose, as was their custom, to plunder the dead, the wounded, and the prisoners. Two individuals, mere boys, seeing me stir among the dead, ran up to me, and one of them put the muzzle of his firelock to my head, to shoot me. I, enraged at his barbarity dashed it away with my fist, and cursed him for a rascal, but he, of course, did not understand me, and he just turned himself round to speak to his comrade, when, at the sound of a bugle, they ran off. This was another hair-breadth escape. Now from this hour until four in the afternoon I can remember nothing; whether from fatigue, and the intense cold, I had fallen asleep, or whether I had swooned from the loss of blood: however, when I came to myself again, I found myself where the men had laid me, with my face on the snow. Where my shattered leg lay, the snow was dyed with my blood. I now sat up to look about me, and found many of my companions on this death-bed were missing. I supposed, though badly wounded, they had, during the day, crawled away to some shelter; but the dead still kept their place. I was exceedingly chilled by the cold, and felt very weak. I could see no person about to call to for help. I remembered I had half a pint of Hollands in my canteen, I dared not drink in the night, for fear of intoxication. This, I thought, would revive my spirits, but, alas it was of no use; my hands were so deadened with the cold, that I could not get the wooden stopper out, it was frozen so hard; neither could I release it with my teeth. What to do next I had to consider. Knowing I must soon perish here, I resolved to try and crawl to the nearest shelter, which seemed like a barn, built with boards. I found I must make an extraordinary effort – it was a life and death struggle. I got two muskets, there being plenty within my reach, thinking I could use them as crutches; but I had much difficulty in rearing myself on one leg, I was so stiff with cold; nor could I grasp them, having lost all feeling in my hands. However, I managed to get the butts of them under my arms, and made a bold step, when they sunk in a marshy place, and I fell flat on my face. After resting, I tried again, but could not succeed; the exertion caused a painful sensation in my breast, my breath failed me, and a faintness came over me. I had no alternative but to try to drag myself along on my elbows and knees. By this means I crawled a little way at a time, and then took a rest to recover my breath. At length I came up to the back of the hoped for refuge, and, to my mortification, saw there was a deep dyke of mud and snow to pass, a high bank to climb, and a hedge to get through, before I could reach the front. Disheartened for awhile, I lay down to consider how to overcome these obstacles. I quickly resolved – it was for life – and flung myself, by one desperate effort, to the opposite bank, thrusting my arm at the same time through the hedge, at the roots;

senior British commander in Bergen-op-Zoom during the assault, Cooke surrendered on the morning of 9 March. See *ODNB*.

there I rested again, holding my broken leg up the while. I found the stakes at the bottom were rotten, and gave way, so that I broke, by the force of my elbows, enough of the hedge to admit my body; with my elbows and knees I contrived to pull myself through. I found myself entering the end of a long street, and, after a rest, crawled round to the front of the building, when, to my surprise, I found it to be a French guardroom. Although I had but small hopes of this place affording me any refuge, I was resolved to try it, though it might only be a shelter for the night. I could see no person about to ask help of, nor could hear any thing, as though all the inhabitants, French and all, had gone to sleep after the last night's ball. I crawled up towards the door, but there lay a worse obstacle still than before. Under the colonnade, and exactly in the doorway, lay, in a heap, about fifty English muskets, broken at the butts, yet with their bayonets fixed on them. At this formidable barrier my courage was about to waver, but that must not be: I looked on that moment as a crisis in my condition, and again resolved to make one other and last effort, by springing over them, if possible, at one leap, from my dead, frozen foot. Not sure that I could leap at all, I feared I might fall on the bayonets; yet the desperate necessity impelled the resolve. I prepared for the hazardous attempt, by raising myself up against one of the pillars of the colonnade, and clung round it till I recovered my breath again. From that position I had a view of the inside of the room; it was large enough to hold sixty men; but, oh! what a horrid sight it presented to my eyes. The guard-bed was filled, jammed together, with the dying and wounded English, and the mud floor was covered with them. They were, probably, some of my companions of the death-bed, as I called it, in the meadow, who had got the start of me while I was asleep, or in a swoon. I observed three French soldiers of the guard, sitting on a bench, before a handful of fire on the hearth. There did not seem to be an inch of room left for me any where, but luckily, as I thought, they all three got up and went away, leaving the bench void. It cheered my spirit. Now is the time, said I, and made the fearful bound, cleared the bayonets, and seized the door frame. I rested here a moment; one other hop, and I made the happy bench; I laid myself down at length, placing my broken leg upon the other, and, with my head on the crown of my cap, I felt a momentary ease; but not the slightest warmth did I feel from the fire; I was too much frozen to feel any slight warmth; I was a mere animated piece of ice. But my comfort was of short duration. A gang of rapacious plunderers came in, and, unmercifully walking upon the sufferers lying on the floor, proceeded to turn over and haul about those upon the guard-bed, half stripping them in search for money, or any thing else. Those on the floor, also, underwent the same painful process. In my turn, three of them set about me, and, in their rough handling, gave me great pain. A fine young man, an officer of another regiment, lay on his back just under my bench, and while one of the villains was standing upon him, he looked up at me, and said, "O, sergeant, this is hard work." I said "We must submissively endure it." However the rascals did not find my money. Having received no pay for many weeks, and being in want of money, I had, but two days before, sold my watch for three pounds ten shillings, all of which I had now in my trousers pocket; this pocket, being very deep, had, in my writhings and from the weight of the silver, fallen from its usual place, so they missed it, and were content to take what they could find in my havresack, such as my case of razors, penknife, inkhorn, and other little matters, also my parchment certificate from the Grand Lodge of Freemasons, the loss of which grieved me. One of them weighted my canteen, and found I had some liquor in it: he relieved me of that incumbrance by loosing the strap and taking it altogether. I asked him to give me a drop, but he took no notice. These went away, but I was not to escape French rapacity so easy. About a quarter of an hour after, I was visited by a party of about a dozen men in arms, having some sort of an officer at their head: I supposed them to be a patrol, or piquet. I judged they had been told about me, as when they entered all their eyes were fixed on me, probably attracted by the glitter of my gold-laced coat. The cowardly officer then motioned me to get up and go with him. I told him, as well as I could, in half French, half Dutch, I was unable, and lifted up my broken leg, which was, at this time, bound by my handkerchief, and covered with clotted and frozen blood. He stood for a while gazing on me then turned to his men, and spoke; when four or five of them proceeded to pull me about, in search of money. Their violence was not to be eluded; and, after severely maltreating me, they found my little bank: the very chink of it seemed to put them all in a mad ecstasy; and it was really amusing to see their antics and gesticulations, in their squabble about the division of my money. They went away, and, a few minutes afterwards, three others came, and searched me again, but finding nothing were going away, when one, with a savage countenance, turned – took out his knife, and seized me, as I lay, by the coat collar. I thought he was going to cut my throat. However, his object was to cut the lace from my coat; and, after cutting a little of it, not knowing its value, I suppose, he went away. I was exceedingly thirsty from the loss of blood, and begged one of the Frenchmen to give me a drink of water, but he disregarded me. I asked another, an old soldier, and, after much hesitation, he took a bucket and went, but a few yards, to the river (an arm of the Scheldt, which passes through the town, and is navigable for small craft), and, as though to aggravate my torture, gave me its salt water to drink. I drank a little of it, and said, "Oh, it is sea water!" when the monster replied, exultingly, in English, "That is more than you would do for any of us in England." I said, "Oh, no, I had had many of his countrymen, prisoners, under my command, both officers and men, and had always behaved with kindness towards them." He said he believed it was a lie. The water made me very sick. The brute gave the salt water to many others, who were also sick from it.

It was getting dusk, and there was no prospect of any thing but death before me. I lay pondering over my helpless condition, while, no doubt, a mysterious hand was working to remove me from this place, though to continue my sufferings in another. As I lay, with my head looking towards the door, a lady and gentleman, arm in arm, were passing, when they stopped to look into this place of woe. Their eyes were fixed on me, and mine on them: I thought I saw commiseration in their

'Wachthuis aan de Boschpoort te Bergen op Zoom' (The Boschpoort Guardhouse at Bergen-op-Zoom). By Joannes Willem Vos after Louis Charles Hora Siccama, 1831. (Rijksmuseum)

faces; I shewed them my bloody leg, and asked them, in the Dutch language, as well as I was able, if they could cause me to be removed to a hospital, or some other place where I might get surgical help. They bowed significantly, and hurried away. In about half an hour after, a man, with a fine white horse and a cart, came and put his hand on me, and motioned to the cart. Hope cheered me up again, but, alas! it was fleeting hope; it was but the removal from one dungeon to another more dismal. My friend, as I might call him, helped me into the street, and set me upon the tail of his cart; he then drove on. It was a very long street, and very roughly paved; and, as my leg was hanging dangling down, the motion of the cart gave me intense pain, as I thought, from the grating of the ragged points of the smashed bone. Here let me be just to one of the French for an act of kindness: an artillery man, who was passing by, saw me writhing in agony, with a quick presence of mind snatched up a soldier's side-arm belt, ran to me, and put it under my foot and over my knee, like a stirrup, and, without any remark, passed on. This act of kindness from one of my deadly enemies, I received with gratitude. It gave me comparative ease.

As I have before shewn, that I was always fond of novel, strange, and interesting sights, I have to relate one here. In riding up this long street, I saw one of the most horrifying and appalling character lying before me. The numbers of the English which had been killed in this street, during the night and morning, had not been removed away, but had just been drawn out of the horse-road, and left lying across the gutter in one uniform row, all the way up the street. Every one of the bodies lay exposed, stripped stark naked. Whether it was the same in other streets, or not, I could not tell; nor for what purpose, or by whom, the brutish exposure was made, unless it might be to frighten the English prisoners, as a warning story, to be told by them when released, and so scare their comrades from meddling with French matters any more. The blood chilling sight, awful as it was, one would think had unnerved me, and made me bless my stars I was not one in their ranks. But, no; I was, by this time, too hardened – too familiarised with the work of human slaughter and carnage, to look even upon this with any other regard than that of a business matter of indifference, in which, for twelve hours, I had then been mixed up.

My racking carriage at length arrived at its destination. It was quite dark, and drew up to the doors of a large and lofty building, which I hoped was a hospital. But, oh, no such luck; it proved to be a French barracks. About the door I saw several English soldiers, in their undress, whom I afterwards found to be prisoners, who had been set to assist and carry in the wounded. Cold reception here, too; my driver had no more to do with me. There he stood; there I sat; nobody offered me any assistance; at last I beckoned to a stout looking man, and asked him to carry me into some of the rooms: he looked very surly, as though he did not like his employ. However, he at last took me on his back as a miller would a sack, and carried me into a very long room, on the ground floor; the gloomy and heart-sickening sight of which was in perfect unison with the rest, and, to any heart less callous than mine, must have been frightfully distressing. My body bearer then, perhaps as callous as myself, with as little ceremony as a miller with his sack, threw me down upon a heap of dead, dying, and wounded – promiscuously mixed up – of French and English soldiers; so that the deadly enemies, a few hours before, were obliged to be quiet bedfellows, and hug each other in the agonies of death. My face, where I lay, came in contact with that of a dead grenadier of the enemy, but I could not tell which face was the coldest. I lay in that position about a minute or so. The man of ours, without speaking, had hurried away. I raised myself up a little to look around on this horrid dungeon of pain and sorrow, and, by the dismal light of a half-dying lamp, quite in accordance with the rest of the scene, I then saw the floor of the large room was covered, from end to end, in one indiscriminate heap. The room contained about twenty-five beds. I mean, by beds, that there were light frames, made suitable for one man, and a sort of bag filled with straw, but no covering. Each bed, in this case, had two occupants; all of them had on their great coats, just as they had been carried in. There were no words spoken – no talk – all were smarting in the bitterness of their wounds, or friendless death. I heard nothing. No sound among this mass, except, now and then, a deep sigh or hollow groan, in giving up the ghost. In contemplating this miserable receptacle of the victims sacrificed to the caprice of Mars, the god of war, I could not help thinking I had but exchanged the death bed I had occupied but two hours before in the meadow, for the horrors of a yawning, ghostly sepulchre. Yet, in all this, my courage and fortitude did not forsake me. I had been half an hour in this tribulation, and no one entered the room. However, hearing footsteps passing rapidly in the passage, and seeing an English soldier, I, with a somewhat commanding air, demanded of him if he had any sergeant there. The man supposing me to be an officer, answered, "Yes, sir." "Tell him to come to me," I said. The serjeant quickly came. I then asked him if I must be left there to perish among the dead; I desired him to have me removed from this miserable place to some other room. He said, he thought the rooms were all full throughout. He went to look, and then told me there was a vacancy at the top of the building. "Take me there," said I. He then got two men to help me up three flights of steps: they would not carry, but merely assisted me. My breath failed me at every half dozen steps, and I had great pain in my breast. They at last got me into a very large room, where my new companions were all of them wounded French soldiers. They laid me on a bed. I asked them if they could get me a blanket to cover me; they said, no, it was impossible. I then asked them if they could get me a cup of warm coffee; but, no, they could get nothing, as they were prisoners. I began to muse on my rather improved situation, but withal it promised to be but a cold and dreary one. In looking around the room, I saw the large sash windows had been all broken during the night; the room having been a firing position of the French, upon the English in the street; whence they, returning the compliment, had smashed the windows. After about half an hour in my new quarters, I heard noisy footsteps on the stairs. I was fearful it was more of my sort; but it was several French soldiers carrying buckets, containing water, sprinkled or tinged with red wine, and others carrying bags with bread. There was some sort of an officer with them; he looked over the room for the English, but there were none but me and a poor boy about fourteen, a soldier in the First Royals; he was next to me. I was very sorry for him; he had a ball through his breast. The officer wrote us down in a book, and then ordered his men to give me a piece of nasty black bread, about a pound, and about a pint of the water and wine. Having excessive thirst I drank it off with eagerness, but my sickly stomach returned it again; neither could I eat any of my filthy bread of this prison allowance, although I had not eat[en] since the afternoon of the day before. The poor boy began to eat his bread, and well for him, as there came a party of villainous French soldiers into the room, who turned me over, and over again, but found nothing but my allowance of bread; that they snatched from me with the acuteness of the jackall, also that from the boy. I thought that being wearied and fatigued as I had been, during the past night and day, I should have got a little sleep this night, but through the screams and groans of the wounded French, and my little companion, I could not. As I lay pondering over my forlorn and doleful condition, I thought of my beloved wife, and endeavoured to cheer myself with the hope of seeing her again. Assured of her sympathy and affectionate help, she would readily bear her share in my adversity.

Next morning, the 10th, the screaming French were removed from my room, to some more comfortable place, but I must remain, cold as it was, and weather it out. About eleven o'clock our prison allowance was brought to us. I drank off my pint of water, as there was no cup left for me to keep it in; but I could not again eat my bread; I had no appetite, and was still sickly. I hid my bread under my bed, and told the boy to make haste and eat his, which he set about, but left part of it, and hid it as I did mine. No sooner had this been done, than a party of rascals came, lifted up the beds, found our bread, and took it away. These fellows were mostly little slim made chaps, with oval visages, and eyes sharp as a weasel's after plunder. My spirit was roused, though I dared not shew it; but I thought, as I lay looking at them – the cowardly villains – in the face, that could I have stood up, I could have whopped any half dozen of them with my fist. How I was to live, without food or surgical help was now becoming a matter of much concern to my mind. Just then a very remarkable incident turned up for my preservation. Lying on my back (and I could lie no otherwise), something had given me acute pain in my loins, which I supposed to have been one of the buttons of my coat lap that was under me.[20] It was, I observed, something small, the size of a button, which had crept through a hole in the pocket, and lodged in the coat tail lining. Not having any feeling in my hands, I asked the boy to get it out. Before I saw it I had hopes that it was shilling, but oh, disappointed hopes, it proved to be a doit, which is about the size of our farthing, but thinner, and in value half a farthing.[21] It had most providentially escaped the jackalls' claws. I had not any idea of this doit giving me relief, and thought no more of it till some hours after, when a little Dutch boy, about six years old, came into the room to play and look at us. My delicate appetite was then craving for some very simple thing, and I thought of an apple, but at that season (March) I hardly supposed there was such a thing to be had. I asked the child if he could buy me an apple with my little all, the doit, calling him to my bed, and making him understand as I thought. Being pleased, he ran away. An hour elapsed and the child did not return. I began to blame my ill luck, supposing the child had misunderstood me and thought I had given it for himself. While musing on my hard lot, and listening to the moans of my poor companion, to my great joy the boy came smiling into the room, with his hat crown half full of little apples, about seven or eight. I teemed them into my cap, and offered my kind little benefactor some of them; with smiling pity he declined them, and went to play again. I next shared them with my fellow sufferer, for which he was very grateful. I eat [sic] the delicious fruit with a devouring relish; the refreshment I felt after it was wonderful; it cheered up my spirits and strengthened my courage, and seemed to be the proper food for me at that moment. Here was a miraculous working of the mysterious hands of Divine Providence for my preservation, while a prisoner

20 Coat lap: that is to say, his rear coat flap.

21 Doit: a small Dutch coin, equivalent to one-eighth of a stiver.

in the hands of the enemy. But none of these marvellous things were then seen by me, through the clouded state of mind I then possessed. I was only assured that the apples, which made me two meals, had saved me from death by starvation. In the afternoon of this day (the 10th) I heard a loud voice at the door of the room, saying, "Are there any of the Guards here?" I thought I should have leaped off the bed with joy, knowing it was the voice of the doctor of the First Guards, who was a prisoner also.[22] I said, "Yes, sir, here is a sergeant of the Coldstreams." (The Second Foot Guards are called the Coldstream regiment.) He said, "What is the matter?" I replied, "I am wounded in the leg." He snatched off a bit of old rug that I had laid over it, when it stunk horribly. He said, very quietly, "Oh, sergeant, this must come off." "I know it, sir," said I; "and the sooner the better. Will you please to do it now?" "I cannot possibly do it to-day," he replied, "I am too tired, and worn out for want of rest, but I will come and do it for you in the morning." He then hurried away. I had again to pass another bitter cold night, anxiously longing for the morning dawn of a memorable day – the 11th of March, 1814.

The morning came, but no doctor: the day passed on till four in the afternoon, when I heard many feet hurrying up stairs; it was my doctor, with two others to assist him, and his sergeant, followed by many of the Dutch people, to see what was going to be done. He said "How do you feel, sergeant?" I said, "Sir, I feel very low and weak, but am anxious to have this stinking leg off." He, smiling, said "He was glad to hear such courage," and began to make preparation. "But sir," I said, "I feel myself in that feeble state, that I fear I shall sink under the operation, unless you will please give me some wine." He said "Well, you shall have some." So he gave some money to a bystander, to fetch me a bottle; but when he brought it, it was a Rhenish white wine and I did not like it: I said, "Let me have the red wine." He sent it back to be changed, and I had red wine. By this time they had got me fixed upon the end of a long barrack table, sitting upright, with my legs hanging down: a bason [sic] was brought for me to drink out of. I said, "Sir, let me have a good draught." He poured out nearly a pint, which I eagerly drank off. In an instant it wrought a wonderful effect, and raised up my spirits to an invincible courage. "Now, gentlemen," said I, "go on, if you please." The sergeant was preparing to blindfold me: "Oh, no;" I said, "I shall sit still, and see as well as the rest." One of the surgeons sat on a stool, to hold the leg steady; the second ripped up my trousers, and took down the stocking low enough; then he waited on the head surgeon. He, with a knife, much like that of a shoe-maker's, took his place at my right hand (it being the right leg to be amputated), the tourniquet being placed painfully tight above the knee; he put his hand under the calf of the leg, and setting the edge of the knife on the shin bone, at one heavy, quick stroke, drew it round, till it met the shin

22 This surgeon, whose last name Jackson gives as Curtis later in the narrative, was William Curtis (d. 1824), battalion surgeon to the 1st Foot Guards. See M.K.H. Crumplin, *The Bloody Fields of Waterloo: Medical Support at Wellington's Greatest Battle* (Huntingdon: Ken Trotman, 2013), p. 209.

bone again. All eyes were fixed on me, but I was too high spirited then to give way. The blood, quickly following the knife, spread around, and formed, like a beautiful red fan, downwards, at the sight of which, the frightened, but sympathising Dutch lookers on, screamed as though they were being cut. They pitied me very much, and said "Poor sergeant-major." Next, the surgeon, with his hand, forced up the flesh toward the knee, to make way for the saw. When the saw was applied, I found it extremely painful; it was worn out; it stuck in the way, as a bad saw would when sawing a green stick. I said, "Oh, sir, have you not a better saw?" He said, he was sorry he had not, as they were all worn out. The bone got through, the next thing to be done was still more painful – that of tying up the ligatures; then followed the drawing down of the flesh to cover the end of the bone, and tightly strapped there with strips of sticking plaster; after this, strongly bandaged: and thus ended the operation, which lasted about half an hour. It was curious enough. These gentlemen, finding me not squeamish, amused themselves by engaging my attention in a conversation, all the time of the operation, about the action during the night and following morning. They then helped me to hop along the room to my bed. I now asked the doctor if he could obtain a blanket for me, which he kindly did. He then looked at the poor boy, and merely put a bit of lint into his wound; bid me good night, and promised to see me in the morning. Having a blanket, I had hopes of getting a little sleep and warmth, but was very uneasy, not having been undressed for more than a fortnight. However, I had some sleep, and, little as it was, it was very refreshing. But here was no comforting cordial to go to bed upon – no sympathising friend – nor so much as a cup of coffee or gruel. The doctor had no power to order us any thing of food. The poor boy and me had finished the last of our apples in the dark, again despairing of getting more food.

The morning of the 12th brought with it new hope, although I had one other pang to suffer from French rapacity. Our prison allowance for the day was again brought us, and, as before, in a few minutes was snatched from us. The poor boy was now fetched away from me. I did not know where he was taken to; but he could not live. Thus, during the three days I had been a prisoner, I had not eat of French bread, or any other food, except the miraculous supply of apples, while the French rascals, no doubt, were revelling on my three pounds ten shillings, and other things. About eleven o'clock, my noble doctor, whose name was Curtis, came bouncing into my room, and seeing me looking cheerful and sitting upright, said, "Well, sergeant, keep your spirits up, I have good news to tell you: a capitulation has been agreed upon between General Sir Thomas Graham and General Bizanet, the French commandant.[23] The prisoners are to be released, and exchanged; and the wounded are to be sent to England, as soon as they are able to be removed." This was cheering news indeed for me, in not only being released from prison, but saved from death by cold and starvation. I then told my kind doctor, whose

23 *Général de Brigade* Guilin Laurent Bizanet (1755-1836), commander of Bergen-op-Zoom's garrison.

name stood high for kindness, how I was and all about how cruelly the French had treated me. He was very sorry for me, and said, "You are a brave fellow; have you got any money?" I then told him what the French had taken from me, and that I had none. Putting his hand into his pocket, he said "You shall have half what I have got, be what it will." He had just ten shillings, out of which he gave me five. I was very thankful. This, I thought, beside the good news, was a glorious God-send; another merciful act of ever watchful Providence, to rescue me from the jaws of death, at this critical juncture of my sad condition: but here, too, I was too blind to see the mysterious hand that was working my deliverance from the hands of a barbarous enemy, and that my body should not make one of the lamentable funeral pile, upon the broad platform of the ramparts ; it being the custom, and, as I afterwards learned, was fact, that the French burned all the English bodies that were killed in the engagement. It was designed that I should be spared to see a more enlightened day (though distant), to give thanks to whom it was due – my great preserver and bountiful benefactor, the omnipotent God.

I had told my doctor I wanted a little nourishing food, but even with money I had no means of getting any, as no one ever came near me to offer me any help. I asked if he could send one of the English prisoners to me, which he did. I told the man, if he would go and get me some white bread and butter, I would give him a shilling. I gave him money, and he said he would try, though he thought he might not have that liberty. However, after a long while away, he returned with it, and a can of coffee. Grand doings I then thought. I gave him the shilling, and begged of him to stop with me while I eat it, lest the jackalls should smell it; this he did. During my meal he entertained me with more good news, viz. that the waggons had already come to carry away the wounded. I prayed him to remember me, as being here alone I might be forgot. He left me, promising he would not forget. I had asked him if he knew to where we were to be carried; he said he thought to Williamstadt, a place where I had been before. Being now well refreshed, but still in great pain, my leg having continued to bleed till all the bandages were soaked and clotted, I laid me down to consider my last move in that unlucky country. One more long and bitter cold journey, of between twenty and thirty miles, and that, too, probably, in the night. Well, all this I did not mind. The hope of going to England, instead of going to France, a prisoner, where I must have died on the way, cheered up my spirits. And, then, in my solitary musings, I thought of the dead, and wished a peaceful rest to the spirits of the departed heroes of this memorable conflict. I consoled myself with my reprieve, and that the means were nigh at hand to finally extricate me from this human slaughter-house – this devouring sepulchre – this charnel-house of old, Bergen-op-Zoom. I was now, in breathless anxiety, waiting for my carriage and four – the waggon, impatient lest I might receive one more last farewell visit from the marauders; but they did not know I had got more money. It was always the vile custom, in the French army, to plunder the vanquished and sack the towns wherever they conquered, which was a strong incitement to the soldiers to be daring and desperate; while the English must respect private property, wherever they go, on pain of severe punishment, and not even to take aught from a prisoner. And, when on the march, a man, for stealing a turnip from a field, would be tied up to the first tree, and get fifty lashes, and then go on.

Hours after passed away and no call for me, till near eight o'clock, when the man, true to his word, came to tell me the waggon had come. I sprung upright, but had yet no feeling in my foot or hands. Two men helped me down stairs. The waggon had a little straw littered in it. The men raised me up to the hind part. I looked sorrowfully on my cheerless bed for the night, without any covering to keep the bitter frost from me, and asked if I could not have the blanket from my bed. "Oh, no," was the answer. I asked for an old pillow to lay my head upon, but received the same reply. A decent looking woman was standing at the door, who seemed to have something to do at the barracks, and hearing her speak English, I beckoned her, and asked if she could possibly obtain for me an old barrack pillow. She said, "If I do I must steal it;" and looking pitifully on me, added, "I will run the risk to get one." She left me, and in a minute returned with one under her apron. I thanked my good friend for her heroism on my behalf, and then took my place at the head of the waggon. Three other poor sufferers were now brought out, and laid on their backs in the waggon; the four just occupying the bottom. Each of them had an amputated leg or thigh, and one or two of them had body wounds also. The drivers slowly moved away, and most heartily glad I was to pass the outer gates of a town containing so vile a den of French thieves: I cannot describe them bad enough.

Long as my narrative has been of this disastrous assault on Bergen-op-Zoom, I might still have enlarged upon it from hearsay information, and, perhaps, with truth, from men who had been engaged in different parts of the fortress, about the town, on the batteries, &c. But I am only desirous of describing the events which occurred relating to myself, and such others as fell within my own immediate observation, and which are to this day fresh in my memory; especially as to what I have said of the cowardly and brutal rapacity of the French upon their helpless and wounded prisoners. But faint, perhaps, is my fractional account of the whole. It may be thought incredible that an army drawn from a nation professing, at that time, to be the genius of enlightenment, could have selected and sent forth such a mass of cruel barbarians that "Polite France" had then located in Bergen-op-zoom. But no great wonderment after all, when one considers their schooling at the feet of Voltaire, Volney, and such like master spirits.[24]

By nine o'clock our drivers had made a few miles way on our long night journey, and being again exposed to the common air, I felt the cold more severe than ever. Through the darkness of the night the drivers lost their way, and by that mishap dragged us many miles round about. The roads, from being wet some weeks before,

24 Jackson is making a disparaging reference to what he deemed to be the hedonistic and irreligious tenets espoused by French Enlightenment *philosophes* (see the Appendix).

and being deeply galled by the wheels of heavy carriages – (having no M'Adam there)[25] – the mud was pressed into hillocks, and congealed to a flinty hardness, were exceeding rough. Some of the wheelruts were a foot deep, through which our waggons had to stumble in and out. I began to think that this journey would quite finish me up, yet I had good courage. What with the cold – the jolting and tossing of the waggon – the soreness of my body – the agonizing pain from my bruised wound, in beating about, I began to be very faint; but here was no remedy save patient endurance. My three poor companions were crying in most pitiable agony. About midnight I found the wheels were running on more smooth ground, like a street pavement, and by and by, we stopped altogether, when I heard a loud voice reprimanding the two drivers for being so long and having lost their way. I knew the voice. It was that of a sergeant of the waggon train, with whom I had had some little acquaintance. I called him by name. He, with a light, got up to the head of the waggon to speak to me, when he exclaimed, "Good God! what a pitiful sight. I am very sorry, Jackson, for your misfortune." As I had got a little money I asked him to get me some warm liquor to drink. He said he had doubts whether he could, but would try. On inquiring our whereabouts, he replied, that we were in the town of Steenbergen. I had before been quartered in this place. We were then about half-way on our journey to Williamstadt. My friend (the sergeant) could not get me any warm liquor; but he brought what was, perhaps, much better for me, a pint of warm milk and a morsel of bread. I sat up and drank it, and it was a great comfort. I looked down at my leg. The jolting of the waggon had made it bleed afresh, and the frost had congealed the blood on the bandages. I asked him if he could scheme a blanket for me, or I should perish in the cold before our journey ended. He said I should have his, though he was on guard, and he gave it to me. It just covered me and the man lying at my right hand. I thanked him, and besought him to try for another, if he could, for the two poor fellows lying at my feet. At this he hesitated; but on my promising the certainty of the driver bringing them back, I prevailed, and so we all got covering. The horses and drivers being changed, the waggon moved slowly out of the town, again to continue our racking journey. I know not whether these drivers lost their way or not, but they kept on till about four in the morning, when they drew up at a large building by the roadside. I called to the drivers to know what they had stopped for. They informed me they were going to bait their horse. The place was a vacant building, which had been made a receptacle for many of the wounded. I asked if there was any fire in the place, and they said there was, upon which I requested them to assist me in getting down that I might warm myself. They set me on a bench before the fire, but I could feel no warmth, so I retired to my racking bed again. We halted about half an hour, and then, at the usual pace, moved on.

25 Jackson is referring to John Loudon McAdam (1756-1836), a Scottish engineer who developed an innovative process known as macadamisation for constructing smoother and more durable roads.

Soon after daylight the waggon again stopped, at a village which I did not know. In a few minutes the waggon was surrounded by the inhabitants, mostly women, shewing much concern for us, and weeping at the sight of our condition, as we lay in the waggon. One would run and fetch us a bit of gingerbread, another an orange, another a piece of bread and butter, and others milk. The kindness of those poor villagers was cheering, indeed, to us all. The next, and last move, in about an hour, brought us to the seaport town of Williamstadt, our final destination. The waggon drove down the main street, as I supposed, spacious and wide, and, as is the fashion in most of the respectable towns in Holland, had a double row of fine trees, forming a beautiful shady promenade, from top to bottom. The drivers then drew up to the door of a very large genteel house, which had been furnished and fitted up with the materials necessary for a hospital, as had also been several other houses. Here was part of a battalion of veterans, who had been brought from England to drudge, and cook, and clean, and wait on the wounded men.[26] I was then taken out of the waggon by some of those, and carried up stairs into a large room, where I found plenty of company of my description, who had got the start of me, but not one of my own regiment – they had gone to some other town.

Here I had the blessing of a comfortable bed, with sheets and blankets, too; a luxury which I had not enjoyed for three weeks – if summed up altogether, during the four months I had then been in that country.

The doctors were, mostly, what are called staff-surgeons, from England, besides the doctors of regiments, but altogether were not half enough. Two of them, old gentlemen, came to look over me, and ordered me undressed. And, oh, when I came to see myself, my body and limbs were just as I have before described the flesh of the Cossacks – crusted with dirt, from lying in filthy places and want of change. They ordered me to be scoured with soap and water, but I begged that that operation might be put off till next day, as my body was too sore from the tossing in the waggon. I then got some comforting food, and as much rest as my pains would allow. Next day I was all the better prepared for the process of my purification. After this I asked the surgeon to remove the painful tourniquet from my knee; but, no, he said that must be endured for several days longer, when my leg would be dressed. The tourniquet is a leather strap, with a hard lump attached to one side of it, about the size of a walnut; this substance is placed over the main artery, and then buckled down very tight above the knee, as I suppose, to stop the blood from flowing too freely. After my cleansing I asked the doctor to examine my hands and foot, as I had then no sensible feeling in either of them; he ordered them to be bathed in spirits of turpentine, day and night, for several days; the right feeling then began to return, and the skin to peel off; that on my foot in large flakes, thick as a halfpenny. My hands became like two bundles of singed rag. In

26 The 1st Royal Veteran Battalion was sent with Graham's force to perform fatigue work and was stationed at Willemstad. See Bamford, *Bold and Ambitious Enterprise*, pp. 63, 105-6.

the course of a few days I had picked off all the dead skin, when my foot became so sore and tender that I could not bear the bed-clothes to touch it; neither could I handle aught with my hands.

I one day got the orderly man to set me upright for a while in bed, and looking over my clothes that lay thereon, I found that I had been touched by many more shots than I knew of; one had passed through my close-coat collar, and cut the black silk kerchief I had on my neck; two others had passed through the lower part of my trousers, on my left leg; and two had passed through my havresack, which hung by my side. I thought after all, I had come off pretty well, seeing that all those shots were harmless. The French had been tolerable good marksmen in the dark, having shot so near the target; but perhaps, and not unlikely, some of them might have been from some of our own men, in the mistakes of the night.

I was very anxious for the day to come for my leg to be dressed, hoping to be relieved of some of my pains. But, oh, when it did come, never shall I forget the intensity of suffering I endured in the first dressing. Military surgeons are not very nice about hurting one. What with tearing off the bandages, which were by this time soldered together with the dried clotted blood, and after them the cross strappings of sticking plaster, which had, as it were, grown to the flesh; the opening of the wound afresh; trying of the ligaments of the arteries; cleansing, and new strapping and bandaging, I feared, in my feeble strength, I must have sunk under the excruciating pain. I thought of the vigour making bason [sic] of wine, at the amputation, but dared not ask for it here. I always thought the cutting off was a minor suffering to the first dressing. After it was over, I had a good many kind words given to me, and a cup of coffee, to comfort me, to go to sleep upon if I could. My other three companions of the waggon, were served the same as I was. The next day, one of them, who had other wounds, with his pains and sufferings went mad, and beat his stump leg to pieces on his bedstead, when four strong men held him down, while he died in his agonies. The other two died in less than a week after; while I was, as it would seem, by the decree of fate, spared, yet to endure a long protracted series of, perhaps, unparalleled sufferings, before I could obtain a cure.

Getting into the month of April, the weather became warmer, but misfortune still hung over me – I was seized with fever. This new enemy, attacking me in my then reduced and feeble state of body, was a source of much concern to my mind: it continued its malignant course for several days till, I believe, the doctors thought it would prove fatal. I was ordered to be removed to a bed placed under a sash window, looking into the spacious street, for air. In this critical situation, when my fever was, perhaps, in its worst stage, and my wound at its sorest, I was one night thrown into indescribable distress, by a tremendous firing of cannon and small arms. The noise in the street and under my window was, if possible, greater than that at Bergen-op-Zoom. Every report was an electric shock to my enfeebled frame, and as a shot through my fevered head. I could not tell what to make of all this. I thought surely the French had pursued us, and, in their turn, were now storming us. I had no one to inquire of, what it was about: none of our nurses were to be seen; and no man that was able dared to look out of the window.

After about two hours of this torture, one of the veterans came into the room, and told us that the Dutch had gone mad on the arrival of the good news of a general peace having been made.[27] This information rather checked my gallopping [sic] pulse, which was going perhaps at the rate of a hundred and forty per minute. I thought this good news of peace all very well for the Dutch, but they would let us have no peace that night, nor did they [the] next day.

Some few days after my fever abated. Singular events were always happening, as in the lottery of my life chances turned up for or against me, though as bad luck would have it, I had always many more blanks than prizes. What to my surprise should now occur, but that my old pay-sergeant should come into the room, who I thought was killed. He had escaped with a wounded arm only. He told me I had been returned missing, and that my gallant captain (Shaw) had sent him [on] a two or three days' journey to seek me, and to present me with some money from him. This was cheering news indeed; especially so in feeling the respect of my officer, and that I should be thought worthy of a present and looking after when lost. That present I knew would produce me many little comforts, as, by bribing the old veterans, I could have something I liked better than hospital allowance. Besides this, I had the pleasure of inquiring after our gallant company, and what became of them after they left me wounded, and were chasing the French from the rampart. He told me the men charged them into their barracks, and then fired through the windows; but soon after (what were left) were taken prisoners. The two poor fellows who carried me away were both killed, or they would have told where they had left me. He then informed me that our regiment was to be quartered in to Antwerp as soon as the French had withdrawn. I felt sorry that I could not go with it, to see the marks of our bombardment.

About this time a letter from my dear wife found me; it was dated a few days prior to the disastrous attack on Bergen-op-Zoom, affectionately describing her uneasiness on my account, in having a presentiment by dream, of seeing me lying wounded and weltering in my blood, and praying that it might not be realised. Alas! poor thing! it was too true. I was unable to sit up, but managed to write her the lamentable answer on my breast, as I lay upon my back.

My fever leaving me but very slowly, I was ordered to be removed to another hospital, a very large old Gothic building, said to have been formerly a royal residence, situate[d] near to the seaside, for the benefit of the breeze. Just before I left, another of those whimsical freaks of chance occurred which marked my career. An officer, who I knew nothing of, nor to what regiment he belonged, came into

27 Napoleon agreed to abdicate unconditionally on 6 April 1814 at Fontainebleau, following which the provisional government in Paris ordered all French commanders to conclude armistices with opposing Allied forces.

the room inquiring for me, holding in his hands my knapsack and great coat; at the sight of which I was astonished – but most agreeably, as I never expected to see them again, after leaving them in the farm yard on the night of the attack. He said he had found them in a church, in the neighbourhood of Bergen-op-Zoom, and seeing my name marked upon them, he had determined to bring them, and find me out; saying that he knew me very well, by seeing me frequently on duty in London. I thanked the gentleman for his great kindness, and thought this was extraordinary good luck. So, now, having my knapsack, containing my wardrobe, laundry, and many other useful things, I could at least change my shirt. After a few days in my new hospital, the fever began to abate, and at length left me. But from the shock my constitution had sustained, by the hardship I had so lately endured, my health was by no means good. The weather by this time was getting hot. I was put into a large room, holding about twenty beds, all of which were occupied with such as myself, on the ground floor, which was paved with flag stones, and was cool and comfortable. My dressings, which had been once in three or four days, were now about every two days. A great many young and inexperienced doctors, or apothecaries, had been sent over from England, to assist in the smarting work of probing and plastering. Some of them were so ignorant that they were frightened at some of our wounds, especially such as mine; and what with their want of skill, and their clumsiness, they inflicted more pain upon their patients, and, at first, did more harm than good. The torturing probe was used in my wound at every dressing.

Two months had now passed away in this place, still I was enduring the painful process without my leg shewing any favourable symptoms of healing. Two of the old experienced doctors took me under hand, and after a long and painful search, said, to my great sorrow, that mine was a very bad case; as the bone had been so very much fractured in the act of amputation, that it could not possibly heal until every particle of it, so fractured, had come away, which would require a work of long time, and for which I must wait with patience. This intimation was most discouraging and grievous, indeed, to me, and I readily concluded that the mischief done was the effect of the worn-out saw. I had now but poor hopes of soon getting well enough to go to England. What with fretting at the unlucky accident, and the sleepless nights I had to endure from unremitting pain, my health was always kept in a state of depression. The sensation of feeling in my stump leg was that of an immoveable weight appended to it; and I very often, in my midnight perturbations, dreamed of a cannon being chained to my leg, and made to march with it so. The old gentlemen doctors would come and operate upon me about once a week, but without any cheering satisfaction to me; as I knew it was not possible for my leg to heal, while it was being continually pulled to pieces with probes and forceps. They treated me, after, with much kindness, and were sorry for my condition; but in all other dressings I was under the hands of the young practitioners. However, to be just, one of them did (though more by chance, I suppose, than skill), after a good deal of torture upon me, blunder out a large piece of the shin bone, about the size of half a walnut shell, at the sight of which I was very glad, and he was very proud. But this was only the first of many more which had to come away, of various sizes. Patience and surgical operations, it seemed, I was then doomed to endure to an indefinite period. It grieved me to see the rapid progress that was making towards healing, in other men's wounds, and mine so tardy; but, then, I considered such grieving to be folly, and so tried to make myself content. We had an excellent chaplain, who always had been with that division of the army to which I had belonged, and who used to hold divine service on the sabbath morning, where it so happened that he could have a church, or some other convenient place, that would hold a regiment. Sometimes we marched into a Protestant church. It was a curious sight to see a whole regiment of soldiers crammed into a small church, every man with his knapsack on his back, and his musket in his hand, at divine service. The religion of Holland, I believed, was, for the most part, of the Romish church; as almost every house I entered I invariably saw their chimney-pieces ornamented with the crucifix. I used, when opportunity served, to stroll into some one of their chapels, but I could not understand their service.

Our excellent chaplain had stationed himself for the most part at Williamstadt.[28] The greatest body of the sick and wounded lying there, he wished to labour among them. He used to come to us twice a week at least, and fixing himself in the middle of the room, performed a short service for us as we lay in bed, and after that a short lecture suitable to our condition at that time, in strains of most affectionate exhortation, solemn warnings, and gentle admonitions. He would usually, in his lecture, take up a pair of crutches and stand upon them, to impress our minds with the helplessness of our condition, the frailty of our nature, and to whom we were indebted for the mercy of being spared to be what we then were, as it might have been our appointed lot to have been of the slain; and, if so, in what condition might our souls have been then. "And where are those of your slain comrades, now?" he would say. But all this solemn and beautiful instruction, I feared, though humbled in our outward condition, was but as seed sown upon a stony rock, and would have no root. There was too much of the rough hardy soldier yet alive in us, and too much of the Holland ice upon our hearts yet unmelted, to allow of any lasting impressions being made, in the way that our kind and good chaplain would have had them. He always finished with a prayer for us, and for our conversion, and furnished us with many small prayer books, with his earnest desire that we would study them. But no sooner is the minister gone, than away goes the seriousness for which he has been labouring to impress our minds, and the conversation returns, soldier-like, to the battle, or to the guard-room tale, to wile away the painful hours.

28 This was probably the Reverend George Griffin Stonestreet, Chaplain to the Guards, or possibly the Reverend Maurice James, another chaplain accompanying Graham's army. See Gareth Glover (ed.), *The Journal and Letters of the Reverend George Griffin Stonestreet, 1814-16* (Godmanchester: Ken Trotman, 2009).

I remember some of the solemn and deeply impressive words of that excellent minister to this day, from one of his sermons on a Sunday, just before our regiment was employed at Antwerp. His subject was on the disobedience of God's commandments, and the awful consequences resulting therefrom. He carried it home to the conviction of every one by the standard of our own obedience or disobedience to our superior officers. "Beginning," said be, "with your corporal, the lowest in command, you all know, who are under him, that you must obey his command, or you are sure to meet with punishment: and next to him is the sergeant; to disobey his commands is to meet with still greater punishment: and if brought before your captain, for the slightest act of disobeying his commands, you, knowing his power to order your punishment, quail under the apprehension of the severity of the punishment he may inflict upon you. And, again, if brought before your colonel, having disobeyed his commands, how erect and orderly you must stand before him – in speechless anxiety – not allowed a word to plead in extenuation of your crime: you feel assured of some heavy punishment, without hope of mitigation. And, higher still, for any act of disobedience of your general's commands: you are not even seen by him or known to him, but on the report to him of your crime, you tremble and quake with fear, looking for some great and extraordinary punishment, amounting perhaps to death. And still greater and higher, if, in your duties, you may be ordered into the presence of the king, how fearful and awing does majesty appear to you, lest you may offend unwittingly; and, petrified with fear, you wish yourself away from the awful presence. And yet you, who must not disobey the command of a corporal, dare, with all the wilful recklessness of the maniac, omit, reject, despise, and set at nought, the commands of the King of kings and Lord of lords, your Maker and Preserver; in whose hand is your life and death, and in whose wrathful indignation the disobedient will be consigned to a punishment that will have no end – eternal!"

To return to our royal hospital. In the month of May the weather became very hot, and fevers were prevailing among us; and, as gangrene was appearing in many of the men's wounds, bad cases were all carried into a field, and put into tents. This had a good effect in saving many. In two or three weeks we were again brought into the hospital. My wound was much improved, and my health also a little. I was longing for the time of our removal to England to come. By the month of June many of the men were pronounced fit to be removed; but still many bad cases, similar to mine, were very lingering. However, in the month of July, after a searching inspection by our old surgeons, they pronounced us all fit to be shipped for England. So the day of embarkation was appointed. I was heartily glad of this, though my health was far from being good, yet I hoped that the sea breeze would refresh me. In my sleepless nights, and mid-watch reflections, casting a retrospective view over my limited tour through this long suffering and oppressed, but now liberated, country – Holland, and what had been my part in it since I had entered into it; what toils and fatigues I was made to undergo; what perils and dangers I had encountered; what hardships and privations I had endured; and the many hair-breadth escapes from death I had experienced, I wondered at myself, how I should be then existing. It was astounding to my understanding, that the bodily strength of a man, aided by his animal spirits, should be alone able to bear him up, and bring him through so many desperate and opposing events, as I had been carried through, such, perhaps, as in a proportionate measure, no other animal in the creation could exist under. But what other power could effect this, save the working of the Divine hand, who had mysteriously decreed it should be so with me. And that I should be spared again to return to my own country, and learn to whom I was indebted for the residue of my life.

6

Embarkation for England

The ship being ready for our reception about nine o'clock in the morning, the whole of the shattered and toppling sons of Mars, in all sorts of forms and shapes, were collected, and the bandaged heroes commenced their short march to the water side; but many of them were obliged to be carried, one way or the other. As for me, as though to mark the procession with respectful gravity, I was carried upon a bier – sitting upright. A novel sight, indeed, this was, for the Dutch to gaze upon, and to shrug up their shoulders as we passed them, in expression of their sorrow for us. I was but in a poor condition for going on shipboard, but was very unwilling to remain any longer behind, as I understood we were the last lot of the wounded in Holland. The distance being no great way, the two men who were my bearers soon delivered me from the dead man's vehicle, on to the quay. Our floating mansion was brought close up to the land; I looked up earnestly at her broadside, as I lay on the ground, and had no favourable opinion of her, as she was not a regular troop ship, but looked like some ugly little trader. I know not what they called her, but I hoped she would be my safe conveyancer. I was then put into a sort of chair made for the purpose, and, by a crane, lifted from *terra firma* (once more to hazard my fate on the treacherous water), poised in the air, like children in a swing-car at a fair, then dropped down a deep hatchway to the bottom of the ship. I was ordered by the doctor to remain exactly under the hatch, for the benefit of the air. Poor benefit I thought I should get of air, from merely a square hole, like the top of a chimney, and amidst the fetid smells of a hundred wounds. But no more viewing the beautiful scenery of the ocean, by moonlight, from the deck. No; I was then stowed into the hold, to enjoy no more sea breeze. I had my old friend, my knapsack, for my pillow, a pallet of straw to lay upon, and a blanket to cover me – and this was my berth for the voyage. As I lay on my back I surveyed our watery hospital with a scrutinising eye, and thought it very much resembled the Scottish smack, which, in coming over from England, had liked to have smacked us into the sea. By about midday all our gallant band of legless, armless, and others something else less, about a hundred in number, were safely lodged round about me, on the bottom of the vessel, and placed like so many packages of goods. So, then, in good hopes, being again committed to the frail care of old Neptune, the god of the sea, and the caprice of Æolus, the god of the winds, we set sail.

The ship, in the afternoon, had scarcely cleared the mouth of the great river Haringvliet, and entered into the North Sea, when, to our sad discomfiture, a gale of wind assailed us, something like, I thought, what I had experienced before, in coming over, and though I could not see the sea, I could hear the effects of it upon the ship. The cracking and, apparently, snapping of the timbers in her sides, by her labouring against the wind and waves, was terrifying indeed. Then I thought Æolus unkind at the beginning, and that I was doomed to bad luck, as though the haggard, Miss-Fortune, with her vigilant scowling eye, was ever pursuing me, wherever I went by sea or by land; for now, in this danger, comes another of a serious character, in a most extraordinary manner. While the vessel was tossing I had liked to have been scalded to death in my bed, where neither hot nor cold water was about me. The cooks had got a large iron pot hanging on a crane, over the fire, on deck, and the ship tossing and rolling in the gale – all hands engaged – no eye to spare for the pot – it swung round upon the crane, over my hatchway, and, at one lurch, emptied half the boiling water down upon me. But, most fortunate for me, I had my eye upon the pot, and, seeing the hot water coming down, I snatched up my blanket over my face, and thus prevented any additional suffering. I called out with all my might, expecting another lurch of the pot, but nothing was to be heard on deck but the gale: at last one of the sick men's attendants ran up and secured it, by fastening the crane. So, by this, I came off with no worse than a hot bath and a fright. I thought then, surely the incidents in my life bore some analogy to those in the tale of Robinson Crusoe; for, like him, I had no sooner got out of one trouble, than I fell into another; only with this difference – his disasters were fictitious, and mine real. And, again, before the gale ended, a sea broke over the deck; our hatch being still open, a drench of cold water next came over us, of which, perhaps, a couple of pailsful came to my share; but this flirt only served to create some merriment in them who had escaped the cooling drench. I had, then, taken both a hot and a cold bath in my bed, almost in the same hour. The ship continued to labour in the gale, more or less, for about two hours, keeping my weak nerves in fretful agitation, fearing lest, as night was approaching, that by some ignorance or mismanagement of the captain we might be cast away; and after escaping the jaws of death in so many forms, I might, at last, find my grave in the jaws of a shark. But ever kind Providence dispelled my fears by ordering it otherwise. The gale ceased; the night became quiet and calm – my mind more at ease; and although in pain, the rocking I had got sent me to sleep on Neptune's bed of uncertain trust, there to luxuriate till it should please the watery deity to send the Tritons, his trumpeters, to rouse me up again; but I wanted no more of their harsh and discordant music. From sleeping soundly I could not tell what passed during the night, but of course all was well.

Early in the morning, my attention was called to the sound – not of the wavy trumpeters – but to the more agreeable notes of the morning breeze, through the mazy cordage of the vessel's rigging. Looking up, through my skylight hatchway, from my bed, I gladly observed a beautiful blue sky, and longed (though to be denied), for the pleasure of being on deck. This day, as did also several following, passed away in very good tempered wind and wave. And our little busy trader, unlike the smack, but faithful, went through her business well, and gaily brought us up to Gravesend. Here, after a short delay, we had to undergo another – yes, another – painful bemauling, in being again wound up from the hold, and reloaded into an open sailing barge; in which, however, I enjoyed myself very much, in the open air, and pleasant breeze of the river. About midday, the sickly band were all re-embarked in the barge, and, under a beautiful and splendid sun, made our way up the Thames. As we neared the city, the strikingly fine panoramic view from my situation, on and off both sides of the river, was, I thought, matchlessly interesting. The noble and vast public and commercial buildings; the numerous splendid domes, towers, and spires of churches; the extensive wharfs and quays; the hundreds of wherries plying the river; the forest of shipping masts; and the wonderful, elegantly built bridges, altogether crowding upon the eye at once, was, to me, grand beyond expression. But, in contradistinction, what a woful [sic] and miserable spectacle must we, the occupants of the barge, have presented to the view of the lookers on, from either sides of the river: some laying this way, and some that; some sitting; some lounging in any form to find small ease from their pains; many of them exhibiting the bandages, like mine, of their stump legs; others with their bandaged arms, off by the shoulders; others of body wounds, having their coats slung by the neck; and again, others, to whom the shot had had no respect, with their faces or heads strapped in crossings of sticking plaster. This, I thought, must have been an appalling sight indeed, to the kind hearted and sensitive Londoners. But, here, amidst the woful [sic] scene I have described – ludicrous enough, to be sure – an officer of some sort, as I supposed him to be (but whether of the sea or land, I could not tell, by his nondescript dress), of gigantic stature, and who seemed to have charge of the barge and its mutilated cargo, mounted upon the highest part of the stern cabin, with his arms akimbo, and wide set legs, shadowing something like the Colossus of Rhodes, spanning a neck of the sea with his legs: or, perhaps, a more happy simile might be taken from the Wellington Achilles, of Hyde Park;[1] the appearance not being inapt, only in the difference, that Achilles has, in his hand, his shield – my officer, his cocked hat. And holding up his broad brim, with Stentorian voice called upon the poor, dispirited, chapfallen heroes,[2] saying, "Now, my lads, give us three cheers." This was just as we approached London Bridge. Three cheers, thought I! What, in the name of

1 Jackson is referring to the Wellington Monument in London's Hyde Park featuring an 18-foot-tall statue of Achilles. Erected to commemorate the Duke's victories, the monument was inaugurated on Waterloo Day 1822.

2 Chapfallen: dejected, chagrined.

all the missing legs, and arms, and eyes, and shattered ribs, can the man, so highly assimulated,[3] be thinking of, to require from the feeble throats of the vanquished, the full chorus of victory? The men, all struck with amazement, turned their eyes to look, but their only response was a low, surly, growl. I, being perched upon a cross beam, nearer to him, he called on me to urge them to cheer: my answer was a contemptible turn away of the head; as surly as the rest; I having no relish to gratify the silly vanity of my new created *fac simile* of the ancient Grecian warrior. However, he, Quixote like, ambitious of fame, with two of the bargemen, set up some sort of a discordant shout; at which the multitude passing over the bridge being attracted, looked down upon the woful [sic] sight below, and were struck mute, and instead of responding to so silly a greeting, lifted up their hands in significant expression of their sympathy and commiseration. Thus we passed the centre arch of the noble bridge. Then, with seeming disappointment and chagrin, our heroic commandant drove the blue-jackets to hurry on the barge,[4] as though ashamed; and so to get rid of his refractory cargo as quick as possible. Passing on our course, in the afternoon we arrived at Chelsea ferry, and there landed: I there found my Achilles was no officer, but the bargemaster. Now, having thoroughly escaped the treachery of old Neptune, and the capricious freaks of old Æolus, and fairly set my one foot on English ground again, I bid adieu to the fabled god, and in solemn thought, gave thanks to my own God, for his merciful preservation, and that the hopes I had in Bergen-op-Zoom, of seeing my dear wife again, were now about to be realised. With this cheering stimulus, and one other last jaunt in a military waggon, over the smooth and level M'Adamised streets of Chelsea, into those of Westminster, I soon arrived at the house of comfort – the Coldstream hospital.[5]

Thus ended my painful voyage from Holland, but alas! not to end my pain, for that was to be continued in its usual intensity to an indefinite period. However, as I had been spared to arrive thus far, I was not only thankful but cheerful, confident that my beloved wife would bear a sympathetic part in my calamity. As soon as it was known how many of the wounded arrived, the hospital became crowded with the wives and relatives of the sufferers, and, of course, much grief was felt and many tears shed on the occasion by the wives. Mine, being a woman of superior mind, after the first momentary shock at the visible alteration in my appearance, recovered herself, and, with more than feminine fortitude, forgot her own feelings in her solicitude for my welfare, and turned to the soothing consolation of encouragement to bear up with manly spirit against the sad misfortune which, by the dispensation of Providence, had fallen to my lot. She had continued at the lodgings

3 Assimulate: to feign or counterfeit.

4 Blue-jackets: that is to say, sailors.

5 The Coldstream Guards hospital was located in York Street, now known as Petty France Street, in Westminster. The site is occupied today by Wellington Barracks, built in 1833, and the Guards Museum.

where I had parted from her, which, fortunately, were convenient for her to visit me, being only two doors from the hospital. The only one of my wife's friends who would deign to visit me was her father, who deplored my loss, and the probable consequences of it in our affairs through life.

After being placed in the able hands of our own surgeons, I anticipated great things, with favourable results, from their well known and skilful practise. As my wound had not been dressed for nearly a week, it became exceedingly uneasy; there not being convenience for proper dressing in our situation on shipboard, and, perhaps, the few young doctors who attended us on board grew tired, and were glad to get rid of us. I was, therefore, looking for a very sharp and very severe probing, and a strictly minute examination into the cause of the delay in not healing.

Next day I underwent the expected smart at the hands of the head surgeon and another. This examination was a long while about, and very painful. Their conversation during the time being in Latin, I did not understand what their opinion was of me, nor was any remark at that time made to me about my wound. In military hospitals it is very different to civil establishments. There is nothing scarcely said to the sick soldier but by stern command; and he is not allowed to ask any question regarding himself; if he does he is sure to be met with the military words of rebuke – "Silence, sir!" He must only answer when asked any question, and submit to all treatment, still in ignorance of himself. This kind of treatment towards me continued for several weeks, without any progressive amendment, when several other doctors were called to see me, and at their painful examination, I heard one of them, in his opinion to another, state that the bone had been so fractured in the amputation, that it could not possibly heal until all the fractured parts had come away, however long that might be. And, furthermore, he added, after all, it might require another amputation above the knee to save life, and which he recommended at once. This dreadful suggestion I thought, as I lay on my back, looking them in the face, was thrown into my ear, as a sort of preparatory intimation to hold myself in readiness, at no distant day, to receive a final order to prepare for the operator's knife and saw a second time. This sad and disheartening intimation to my mind, which had, up to that time, been hoping better things, preyed on my spirits, and my health began to give way. I was ordered to be an out-patient; being able to go upon crutches, I might take air as I chose, in Birdcage Walk, into which the back part of the hospital opened. This order I liked very much, as I could thus enjoy the society of my wife, and the comforting benefit of her kind attentions at our lodgings, and also easily attend the hospital at dressing time every morning. Under this treatment for several weeks my health improved, but still my wound exhibited unfavourable symptoms. After a little exertion on my crutches it would become much inflamed, which, to my sorrow, shewed it to be unsound, and still a bad case. I dared not tell the doctor of it, lest I should be ordered into the hospital again. However, I could not long conceal it from him, when he ordered me in, and to lie in bed as before. This was very mortifying, especially as I was dreading another amputation. A crowd of distressing thoughts were constantly harassing my mind, in anticipation of a new operation.

In this lamentable condition, the doctors were continually searching after, and extracting small pieces of bone from the leg; and thus it went on with me until February, 1815, when more favourable symptoms of healing began to shew themselves, and again I was made an out-patient. Thus, after several weeks more had passed away in flattering hope, my health again rallied, and the wound rapidly healed to a mere speck; and having heard no more about a second amputation [for] so long, I was in full hopes of my painful sufferings being at an end, and that I should soon expect my discharge. And now, to cheer my spirits, a most unlooked for circumstance turned up in my favour, promising me great things; but, like many other promising phantoms, in my unfortunate lot, it proved a delusion. It was this: a man whom I did not know came to my lodgings, saying very abruptly, "Sergeant Jackson, you must come with me to the commissary general's office; there is a place for you as a clerk."[6] "For me," said I, "who could have recommended me[?]" "I don't know," he said, "I am a clerk there, and I am sent for you; go with me directly – it will be a good thing for you." I said, "I am not fit to be seen in that office upon crutches." "Never mind," he said, "you will do without them some day." So I cheerfully went with him; and when I arrived at the office, in Downing Street, there was no question asked me; but a stool was placed at a desk, and a gentleman laid before me several large forms of returns, to be filled up, all of which I found no difficulty in doing, and which gave satisfaction to my employer. On returning home that day, my wife and I were rejoicing greatly at my promising good luck, as it might lead to permanent employ under government for life. Two other days passed under the same impression; but, oh, it was not to be so – there was treachery in my path. The distance I had to go from York Street, Westminster, to Downing Street, was about half a mile, three times a day: swinging on my crutches, was very fatiguing; consequently from that over exertion, my wound became exceedingly painful, and frightfully enflamed. I went to shew it to the doctor, he looked at it with a sort of frowning perplexity, and without any remark, after hesitating a few moments, snatched up a piece of burning or solar caustic, and rubbed it all over the surface of the wound. The torture was dreadful. He then said, "Now go up stairs and go to bed." I then, with aching heart as well as aching leg, went and took up my old quarters as before. I found many of my former companions were missing, some by death, and some by discharge; but many still remained, their cases being as bad, and some worse than my own. As I did not return home, my distressed wife suspected what was the cause, and was very unhappy. She was not allowed to

6 The offices of the Commissary-General of Stores were at that time located in Parliament Street, Westminster, near Downing Street, while the offices of the Commissary-General of Musters were at the Horse Guards. See for instance *Essays on the Theory and Practice of the Art of War* (London: Phillips, 1809), vol. III, p. 398.

see me until the proper visiting day. The man in waiting brought me a poultice for the night,[7] and the next morning the whole of my wound was all undone, and as completely opened again as it was at my first dressing in Williamstadt. I thought still misfortune would never cease to persecute me, at home as well as abroad, and that this new and unlooked for calamity and its probable consequences in long suffering, would put a period to my existence.

On the visiting day my poor unhappy wife came to see me and bewailed our hard lot, but still used all her affectionate endeavours to soothe, comfort, and encourage me to fortitude and patience, in bearing the painful process I had to undergo. The second doctor, who used to attend the men in desperate cases, was a big muscular man, very clever, but had not the most tender heart for his suffering patients. He would, with his powerful grip, take hold of my leg, and squeeze it till he made the blood fly out of it at the end, and if I happened to quail at the pain I was suffering, he would look me frowningly in the face and say, "Do I hurt you?" If I answered with a feeble affirmative, he would say, "I am glad of it." But if a man stood his dressing well, he would be rewarded with some extra diet. Now I had to endure more of the nine-inch probe than ever. That instrument and the forceps were for several weeks in daily practise upon me. The probe, every time forced up to the very joint of the knee, especially the under part, until, by the repeated irritations of those parts, it caused an enormous abscess to form under the ham, extending largely upwards. The pain, during its formation and enlargement, was indescribably severe, and had to be endured for a fortnight. My doctor then, with a sort of hook-pointed pruning knife, made a deep incision on the inside of the knee, and another under the ham, in which he cut the main sinew, so that a piece of it, like the first joint of a little finger, afterwards came away. Dashing his two forefingers into the apertures he had made, he crammed them full of hurds to keep them open.[8] Being exhausted after this painful endurance, he gave me some momentary stimulus, and bid his man look after me and give me some good diet.

Now lying in bed and being in such excruciating pain, my health again gave way. In the month of April the weather was very hot, when, as though my measure of suffering was not full to the brim, I was seized with a malignant fever, which, in a few weeks, so wasted my body, that I became a frightful skeleton; and so light had it become, that the waiting man who had to move my bed would put his two hands under my back, and carry me to another with the ease of a nurse carrying a child. I thought surely I was in the jaws of death for the last time, or, if I recovered, it would be a greater miracle than any I had yet known. Although my health, and strength, and appetite, were quite gone, yet I felt a wonderful courage within me. I had several doctors daily (and oftener) to visit me, and from what I could

7 Poultice: a soft and moist mass of material, usually plant matter or flour, kept in place with a cloth and applied to the body to relieve soreness and inflammation.

8 Hurds: the coarse parts of flax or hemp, also known as hards.

judge by their manner, they considered my case hopeless, especially as it was usual in extreme situations like mine, to tempt the appetite. I was told, in kind words, to think of what I should like to eat or drink, and whatever I fancied I should have. I wanted no more of mortal food or drink; I considered that my days were numbered, and that the last was at hand. A kind minister of the Church of England attended the hospital twice a week, who seemed much interested in my awful situation: he would come and kneel at my bedside, and endeavour to comfort me with the hope of eternal life, through the precious blood of my Redeemer, and never left me but with his prayerful commendation to the mercy of God. In all this extreme weakness I retained my perfect senses, in calm and tranquil resignation. My dear wife was sent for to see me, as it was thought, for the last time. Of course it was a distressing interview. She took a last farewell, as she, and I too, then thought. But, wonderful to myself, that there should be such remarkable wavering in my destiny; that I should escape death in so many forms, and still be reserved to encounter new miseries; as though He who only has power over death had said, "Thus far shalt thou go and no farther. Let him alone a little longer." Then followed an interesting event, the recital of which may not be credited, but it is a fact. Next morning – it was a crisis – as I lay on my back, musing on my awful situation, just at break of day, and the bright sun was looking on my bed through the sash above me, and every one in the ward were fast asleep but myself, perfectly clear in my intellects, I beheld a spectre! I remember it well while I describe it. It seemed to rise gradually from the floor at the foot of my bed, shewing a full bust from the waist upwards, and exhibiting to my view the figure of an aged and venerable looking man, with a grave and reverend countenance; eyes rather piercing, but without terror; the face furrowed and lined as that of a very old man; his beard quite white, thin, and irregular, as though some had fallen off here and there, with but little hanging below the chin; his hair perfectly white, thin, and irregular, but the head not bald; the face altogether pale and ghastly. He was covered with a loose white robe somewhat similar to a priest's surplice, his arms being hid in the folds. In the position I lay, with my head rather high, I had a perfect view of the figure. I felt no alarm, but was perfectly collected and unmoved. The figure remained in that position a few seconds, with its eyes fixed on mine, and mine on his. Then, in a mild, but solemn tone of voice, audibly said (so that a man in the bed near to mine might have heard, if awake, the words which seemed to fall from the figure), "You are not to go yet!" It then began gradually to sink, as though it were, into the floor, keeping its eyes on mine till it disappeared altogether. The apparition from first to last remained about half a minute. This I thought something very extraordinary. But, wonderful to relate, from that hour, the fever began to subside, and my recovery afterwards was very rapid.

I made no mention of this circumstance to any but my wife, who was exceedingly rejoiced at the unexpected change in my condition. She thought the apparition was an illusion, arising from the weakness of my head – but I was quite sure of the contrary. When the doctors came to the hospital at eleven o'clock, the first inquiry was, "Is that sergeant dead?" Being answered in the negative, they flew up stairs, and with evident surprise one took up my hand, instantly saying, "He is better – he is better." Then, after as little punishment in dressing as he could help, my doctor asked me how my appetite was, and if I could fancy any thing in particular: I chose boiled chicken and a little wine and water. I had it, and felt so refreshed after it that I fell into a comforting sleep, such as I had not had for weeks before. In this progressive state of recovery I became much affected by the sickening smells of the ward. My doctor ordered me to be removed to a small barrack, called the recruit house, where I should be quiet, and in the fresh air. As I was not able to stand on my crutches, I was carried down stairs, and once again placed on the bier (not sitting upright as in Williamstadt), but in this case I was laid on a mattress; the distance being about five hundred yards to my new abode. As I rode along on death's palanquin,[9] I thought how singular it was that things should so concert together as to bring me so often into contact with death; one with a mind of more sensibility than mine at the time, might have sunk under his awful menaces. Arriving at the recruit house, and carried up three pairs of stairs, I was lodged in a small airy room to myself, looking into the Green Park. This I thought a great comfort, though I kept my bed. But there, too, in that pretty solitude, I was not to have all the peace I hoped for; in my then state of weakness I had to endure one other racking annoyance from fire-arms. An extraordinary national rejoicing then took place, for the victory of Waterloo. The chief scenes were in the lower and upper Green Parks; the lower was occupied with a display of the most magnificent fire-works that could be conceived or devised, with some other loud explosions which I did not understand, besides firing of cannon at intervals. This was, indeed, distressing to my fevered head. I could see, as I lay in bed, rockets, by hundreds, sent up; and serpents, by thousands at once, were shot up to an enormous height, by some explosion from large upright cylinders for the purpose, filling the elements with one mass of hissing blaze, and producing a feeble roar of thunder by their numerous explosions: those doings continued till morning. But that was not half the noisy work to be done. In the upper part of the park a sort of sham town had been erected with slight boards, for the amusement of the public during the day; and about midnight a regiment of soldiers formed in it as a garrison, then another regiment came to assault and take it by storm; and, to give it a more terrific appearance, they fired the town. The sham work was no doubt performed in grand style, and, still better, there were no waggons wanted to carry away the wounded. Had I been all well I should [have] liked to have been one of the parties. The light cannonading and rattling of musketry, and their alternate mock shouts in their charges, for about an hour, were rackingly annoying to me, and brought up into my recollection all the horrors of the disastrous night in Bergen-op-Zoom,

9 Palanquin: a covered litter for one passenger.

which caused me then to be lying on that bed. I then fully hoped that it would be the last gunpowder disturbance I should ever be troubled with.

Soon after this, as I got down stairs into the Birdcage Walk, to bask on the sunny bank under the trees, my health and strength rapidly improved, and my wound also healing quite sound, I was again made an out-patient, when my doctor told me, I had no need to fear that it would trouble me any more. It was then the seventeenth month that I had been suffering torturing pain, whereas it ought to have been well, at most, in six months. But all this extra suffering was owing to the working of the bad saw, in the amputation of the limb, at Bergen-op-Zoom. Being seen about again upon my crutches, and getting well, it seemed as though I was become a nuisance on the muster roll, and must be got rid of at any rate. Being useless, I was, of course, no longer worthy to eat the king's beef. My discharge was then filled up, and brought by the head clerk for my signature. This document was expressive of my having received all pay, arrears of pay, and allowances of clothing, &c. This I was to sign, and next day go to Chelsea, to pass the board, as it is called. Knowing I had a good deal of back pay, and some allowance for clothing, due to me, I refused to sign the document; the clerk urging, saying, whatever was due, would be sure to be sent after me into the country; but still I refused: so he reported me to the commanding officer, who ordered the quarter-master to investigate my grievance. I had kept my own account of what was my due, and presented it. The quarter-master, whose name was Worrad, a native of Walsall,[10] said I had done right, as, if I had signed, I had no more claim, and might never have got my dues. He said he must write over to Holland, where the regiment then was, to prove my account. That detention kept me on the mess-roll about a month longer. Mr. Worrad had been one of the sergeants of the Coldstream regiment. He was an old soldier, and had been wounded in Spain. When I entered the Guards he was quarter-master-sergeant; and, for his military tact and meritorious conduct, was commissioned to the rank and title of quarter-master-captain. He went out with us in the expedition to Holland, and was well beloved by the soldiers. His business was to provide rations for the regiment. If the commissary of the division had failed to obtain a supply, Captain Worrad would have it, if it was in the district. As we happened to be located near the enemy, provision dealers were fearful selling, lest they might afterwards meet the vengeance of the opposing army. But the plan he adopted was this: he would find out where there was provisions; then he would take a party of armed men with him, and others on fatigue, with a couple of light waggons, and

10 George Warrod (rendered 'Worrad' by Jackson) was indeed born in Walsall. A plater by trade, he was discharged from the Coldstream Guards aged 45 on 6 November 1818 after 25 years 187 days of service, including more than eight years as Quartermaster-Sergeant. The cause of his discharge was noted as 'infirm[ity] from long service.' Warrod was never commissioned as a captain, as Jackson implies, but did serve as the 2nd Battalion's acting Quartermaster. See TNA, WO 97/215/157 and Glenn Steppler, 'The Coldstream Guards at Waterloo: A Quartermaster's Tale', *Journal of the Society for Army Historical Research*, vol. 67 (1989), p. 66.

request to purchase. The Dutchman would refuse to sell. The captain would then put down, in money, the full price, and order his men to seize upon it. Thus, but for Captain Worrad's resolute perseverance, we should have gone many a day without food, in our miserable cantonments.

In the interim of waiting for the settlement of my account, my gallant captain (Shaw), who had got well of his wounds, hearing of me getting well, sent his servant to bring me to his house, when he kindly presented me with a cheque on his banker, for five pounds, as he said, to buy me a new leg with. This I thought was my best healing up plaster. Some while after this, and being, contrary to usual, just for a moment in luck's way, what should next occur, but the commanding officer gave me a note of recommendation to the Humane Society of London; when, after some questioning by those gentlemen, and their sympathy for my case, I was presented with the sum of fifteen pounds. This was cheering indeed, and glorious news to go home with. Next was the arrival of my returns from France, proving my account to be correct, amounting to better than ten pounds, which I received, and then, having signed my discharge, I was ordered to go to Chelsea, as in another week a Board day would be held. So in the month of August, 1815, entering on my thirtieth year, away I went on my crutches.[11] When I appeared before the Lords Commissioners of the Board, they eyed me up and down, and seemed to consult for a moment, when one of them said, "Oh, he is a young man, able to get his living." No questions asked me, but at sight, I was knocked off, with the pitiful reward of one shilling per day – a mighty poor recompense, I thought, for having spent twelve years of the prime of my manhood in the service of my country; lost the benefit of my trade during that period; and, worst of all, crippled for life by the loss of a limb. Having then no more use for my scarlet coat, I set my wife to cut off the lace, and that, together with the chain and tassels which ornamented my cap, she sold for thirty shillings.[12] I then bought myself a suit of plain clothes, to hobble my way with into a new sphere of life, among new beings, and, as it were, into a new world again; there to seek, though, with but a doubtful prospect, a new fortune. I then bid eternal adieu to war, with all its turmoils and disastrous results – its infernal machinery, and the diabolical use of it, invented for the destruction of man, in the hope of spending the residue of my life in peace. I might never have been a military man but through the adversity of the times in those days when I entered the militia; and should perhaps never have gone farther had I not been driven by the tyranny of an adjutant; driven into war after that was a matter of course; thence driven by misfortune into the humiliating condition of a cripple; and

11 Thomas Jackson appeared before the Chelsea Board on 8 August 1815. See TNA, WO 116/19. At discharge, Jackson was noted as a buckle maker by trade, five feet nine and a half inches in height, with brown hair, hazel eyes and a fresh complexion. For his pension record, see TNA, WO 97/181/59.

12 Sergeants in the Foot Guards sported gold lace on their coats as well as gold cap cords and tassels.

driven by cross-purposed incidents through life up to that period, I knew not to what next I was to be driven, but cheerfully hoped better things.[13]

After passing the Board at Chelsea, I had one other march to go upon my crutches, and that was a visit to the maker, to be fitted out with what is vulgarly called a wooden leg, but which, in reality, is a knee-crutch, upon which I was to make my way through life in regular slow time, but to halt as often as I liked. This new appendage of Chelsea renown was to be free of cost – without money – without price; a free, gratuitous, national gift. Ought I not to have been very grateful? Somehow or other, at that time, I was not grateful. Never shall I forget my unceremonious installation into this novel piece of furniture; this curiously wrought, though ill shaped, piece of timber – this "National Testimonial" – this trophy of war, which I had won by my deeds of arms. When fitted on, strapped by the knee, and girt at the waist to painful annoyance, I looked down in sullen silence at the hated appendage, with about the same kind of satisfaction which a dog does when he gets a tin kettle tied to his tail: ashamed, he runs into the first hiding-place he can find to gnaw it off. I tried to view it in a better temper, but could see no comeliness in it, and, after all, denounced it as making a personal deformity, from which the eye of the proud recoils with scorn. It is the coarse joke of the vulgar; and the sport of impudent children. These remarks never fail to be realised; by them the luckless veteran is wounded afresh in the more sensible part – his feelings. For him none have sympathy; he sees himself an isolated being; the gaze of all, he is looked shy upon; he may be friendless: he is, like an outcast of society, treated with proud contumely,[14] as the offscouring of his race. And for what? He has degraded himself in their eyes in having been a soldier. The very tag-rag of the town,[15] who would much rather live by thieving than by soldiering, will reproachfully say, "O, he's an old soldier!" In this moody vein of reflection the once gay and glittering sergeant of the Royal Guards sees and feels a sad reverse. He, who, in his Light Infantry discipline, had been trained to the fleetness of the roebuck – to dash through the forest jungle – to leap the water brook – to bound the hedge fence, or vault the field gate, and made to escalade the scarp wall of the deadly fortress ditch, rush up the glacis, and beard the enemy on his rampart[16] – is now cut down in his bloom; humbled, dejected, dispirited; logged by the leg for life to an ugly, odious piece of timber. But let him try to console himself under so

13 A footnote in the original text reads as follows: 'It was not my lot that I should go with my regiment to share in the honour of the victory of Waterloo, where, perhaps, I might have fared worse than I have. But, having the general returns, I just mention the Coldstream loss, which was 310 killed and wounded. The British loss altogether was 11,116. Hanoverian, 2,960. Dutch, 4,136. Prussian, 33,132. Making a total of 51,344.' The 2nd Battalion of the Coldstream Guards indeed fought at Waterloo, distinguishing itself in the defence of Hougoumont.

14 Contumely: insolent or insulting language or treatment.

15 Tag-rag: the lowest class of people or rabble.

16 Beard: to boldly challenge or confront.

disastrous a reverse, by the remembrance of his country's presentation of, not only a new timber toe every three years, but in having been put in the receipt of one shilling per day for life. But all this he may perchance lose, should he not keep the, not military now, but the *moral* step.[17] So with this, his allotted compensation, let him sit down and smoke his cigar; and if his pipe is not quite put out let him try to sing, if he can, the two first lines of the old corporal's song, as they stand thus–

"Who'll serve the king? says the sergeant; huzza!
Roll went the drum, and the fife play 'd merrily."[18]

Oh, no. Harmony to the old soldier has become a dead letter. His martial music – "The spirit-stirring drum, the ear-piercing fife,"[19] the band of inimitable strain, so proudly stepped, has no longer inspiring charms – the attractive spell is broken. Nay, perhaps the laughed at shell, exploding over head, would not again so much as raise one smile in his thin-jawed pallid cheek.

But why all this sullen, surly soliloquy—this ridiculous quarrelsomeness with the new bandalorum? It being a very good make shift. Although my kind hearted captain gave me five pounds to buy a real, handsome, well shaped, rightabout leg, yet the Chelsea timberonian is a far better thing to get about with! So I thought, what was the use of being ill-humoured and making a fuss about it, but put the best foot foremost, and make the best use of it; and as there was no better remedy than good-tempered patience, it would be just as well to be merry as sad. And although I could not very well then fall into choral concord with the old corporal's song, still it might be somewhat *apropos* in telling the words of an old song, truly characteristic of the good-heartedness of the Old English Farmer, on seeing a poor, discharged, wounded soldier marching on his crutches.

"As a jolly old farmer sat soaking his clay
At the door, by the side of his dame,
When a poor old soldier by chance came that way,
Worn out with fatigue, and quite lame:
Said the farmer, 'Friend, stop, and here you shall find
That I'm willing, with heart and with hand,
To relieve such as you – and, dame, to him be kind,
For he is one who has guarded our land.'

17 Veterans could lose their pensions due to criminal convictions. See John Cookson, 'Alexander Tulloch and the Chelsea Out-Pensioners, 1838-43: Centralisation in the Early Victorian State', *English Historical Review*, vol. 125, no. 512 (February 2010), p. 72.

18 As noted previously, this song first appeared in the 1807 comic opera *Two Faces under a Hood* written by Thomas John Dibdin with music by William Shield.

19 This quotation, frequently used in Napoleonic-era British soldiers' memoirs to describe the emotive power of military music, is from Act 3, Scene 3 of Shakespeare's *Othello*.

"'Step into my cottage – your spirits I'll cheer –
Dame, bring the poor fellow some food,
And draw him a jug of our best home-brew'd beer,
And let's try how to do him some good.
And, when he's refreshed, he will shoulder his crutch,
And shew how in battle they stand:
Let us do what we can, for we can't do too much,
For one who has guarded our land.'

"Now the soldier refreshed, once more he revives,
And begins of those days o'er to tell;
How many brave comrades of his lost their lives,
And how they all gloriously fell.
'Huzza!' said the farmer, 'it ne'er shall be said,
My heart don't with feeling expand;
This brave fellow shall ne'er want a morsel of bread,
For he is one who has guarded our land.'"[20]

Would to God there were more sensitive hearts, such as the above pathetic lines describe the farmer, and fewer lame soldiers!

20 This song, most commonly known as the 'Jolly Old Farmer', is also sometimes titled 'The Wounded Soldier' or 'He's one who has guarded our land'. Although the author is unknown, the song probably originated during the Napoleonic Wars and appears on several printed broadside ballad-sheets from the first half of the nineteenth century held by Oxford's Bodleian Library. See *The Universal Songster* (London: Fairburn et al, 1826), vol. III, p. 229 and the Bodleian's Broadside Ballads Online (ballads.bodleian.ox.ac.uk).

7

Discharged - Leaves London for Walsall

Having now done with all sorts of military paradings and doings, and becoming somewhat more reconciled to my new appendage, and seeing, as the old adage has it, "That what must be, must be," after applying to the commissary's office about my place, which then was filled up, I at once turned my thoughts towards Staffordshire, and of necessity to my native town. After making the best of all things, but still preserving my old friend, my knapsack - the comforter of my weary head, after the toilsome day in the frozen region - about the latter end of August, my wife and I took our place in a night coach, and away we went. Arriving at Walsall the next day, I found my parents still living, but [they] were aged, infirm, and unable to work, so as to get a good living, consequently they were in poverty and in need of help, rather than looking to for help.[1] However, I did not need any help, but had the means to comfort them a little. They received us with parental affection, and, of course, lamented my misfortune, and its probable consequences in future, by disabling me from working at my trade. After a week or two in holiday at home, we must then take and furnish a little house, to try how prettily we could live upon a shilling per day, with provisions ranging very high at that time; we did so; but very soon found that, leg or no leg, I must go and try to get work at something. One day that I was going about the town for that purpose, I met with the first cutting insult on my misfortune, such as I had anticipated to be realised by the vulgar in my own town. In passing a group of the unwashed, assembled at an idle corner, as they all gaped on me one said, "Ho's he?" Another answered, "Why don't yo know him? he's young Jackson, as went into the militia, and then he must volunteer to go and see war, and they'n sarved him out for it." "Sarves him right," says another, "he had no business there." So this was a specimen I had, of the sympathy of that brutal class of the grimsy scum of that day. Returning home unsuccessful, I was rather out of temper with the barbarians, but resolved not to mind them in future. How sensibly cutting to the suffering object who had shed his blood in the common

1 Thomas Jackson Senior, the author's father, was still living in Dudley Street, Walsall for the 1821 census and was described as a 'pauper'. See French, *Thomas Jackson*, p.21.

cause for their general welfare. In contrast, the gentlemen of my town had for me, always, a kind and sympathetic word, and were ready to do me any good.

In the month of November of this year (1815), and being as it was in the beginning, that all things natural should go on in the usual regular way, amongst the rest it was the part of my beloved wife to present me with a son, which, of course, had a little mouth, and would soon lay claim to a portion of my national allowance, and thereby be more urgent on me to bestir myself.[2] The trades of the town were generally good, except that of my father's, which had been superseded and nearly annihilated; but the casting part of it, which I had from a boy been used to, was one of the best trades going for a good workman. This branch forming the basis of many other trades in iron ware, at which I could have had constant and regular employ; but, alas! for my misfortune, it required both that power of body and activity of limbs which I had been deprived of. This disappointment was of course very grievous; so I could only add it to the lamentable catalogue of crosses and losses in the book of misfortune. In that scarcely never failing trade, many a smart property has, to my knowledge, been gathered by persevering men, while I have had to deplore the cause that debarred me of the same privilege. I had, then, to wander about on my Chelsea heart-of-oak, alone – through solitary fields and lanes – straining my wits how to procure a future living; like a friendless outcast, no one cared for my applications, as though my mutilated appearance told against me. But just upon this, and, as the old adage again has it, "It is a long lane that has no turning," I happened to have a younger brother who had been brought up to a light branch of the plating trade, such as bridle buckles and other small articles; which trade being good, and work then well paid for, seeing my very humbling condition, he kindly offered to teach me to work at the same. I rejoiced at the offer, and set to work. I was not altogether at a loss in using some of his tools; but of course I could not, for a time, ask for any wages. The trade keeping good, and plenty of it, with my health good and spirits up, and with untiring perseverance, I made such progress as to be able to earn, in the space of six months, twenty shillings a week, but a full workman would earn his thirty. In this happy event, and the hope of its continuance, I began to promise myself many fine things in well doing. Finding the labour so light that I could, alternately, sit down and stand up, I thought I could not have had a more agreeable trade. But, oh! here, too, my new raised hopes and vain promises, like many of those behind, were not to be realised – another "crook in the lot" was at hand.

One of those commercial panics arrived, which have, in my time, periodically visited our country, causing ruin to merchants, bankers, and chapmen[3] – insolvencies among every class of manufacturers – and, consequently, distress inconceivable among the working classes. Both the home and foreign trade rapidly

2 Charles Jackson was christened at St Matthew's Church in Walsall on 25 December 1815.

3 Chapmen: peddlers, itinerant salesmen.

died away: that of mine, being altogether home trade, instantly stopped. These panics would range over two or three years, before any revival of trade. The tools of our shop being all rusty for want of use, and I, being willing to get a shilling at any work, turned my hand to filing iron buckles, and other things; but this little help soon vanished under the panic. Nothing to do for a long time, I had again to wander the solitary fields and lanes, at my wits end as to what course I should take. All provisions were enormously high. We were often driven to the scant of one meal a day. The workhouse overflowing with the families of the working classes; and hundreds of others just kept from starvation, by being employed upon the highways, in breaking stones and mending roads, at one shilling a day, paid out of the parish rates. This miserable state of things continued to go on unabating. Men then maddened with the desperation of their case, began to reason upon the cause of their calamity, turned their minds to the study of dangerous and wrong-headed politics, attaching all the blame to the misgovernment of our rulers. When clever designing men seized the opportunity of disseminating all sorts of inflammatory publications throughout the country, fraught with pernicious disaffection, inciting to revolution. By such means as these a continuous agitation was carried on, up to the carrying of the Reform Bill.[4]

Still hoping better things in the mysterious future, who could have dreamed that, under the very promising circumstances in which I had been placed, with every prospect of getting a comfortable living, should soon after be driven by that untoward event, the trade panic, to the necessity of pledging our clothes to buy food. Surely, I thought, some evil angel, ever watchful, stood in my way, to cast a withering blight over all things promising me prosperity. This state of murmuring misery went on with me to near the middle of 1817, when again the interposing and wonderful mysterious hand of Divine Providence came to my relief, in a way most unexpected, and continued with me through several successive years, for which I was very thankful. This was the way it came about: I had a first cousin who was the wife of a[n] innkeeper in the town; she was rather distant, and, as I thought, had no regard for my humbling condition; however, she had an acquaintance with a young lady, who was the daughter of a coal merchant, who was doing a large scope of business – in amount, probably, to four thousand a year. The coal merchant's clerk dying suddenly, and one to take his place being wanted immediately, my cousin, without any knowledge of mine, kindly made application for the situation for me, through her friend, the daughter. I was, as may be supposed, on being sent for, most agreeably surprised, on being informed I was to go upon trial. When I came to the office I found a set of double entry books, which had been well kept by the late clerk; but as I had been used a good deal to military books, with all their intricacies, I did not find much difficulty in keeping those of

4 The Great Reform Act, officially the Representation of the People Act of 1832, amended the electoral system in England and Wales by extending voting rights and abolishing rotten boroughs.

the coal merchant. Beyond this, as it was a very great trust – integrity, steadiness, and common honesty only were wanting. All this I knew I could command. I had to keep account of all stock bought in, and of all sold out; to receive all moneys; and pay all bills, wages, &c.; to make up my cash book every week, and deliver up the balance. The next thing was to agree for terms. The crafty old gentleman, knowing I had a pension and being out of employ, bantered me down below the terms of his late clerk; however, rather than await the casual chance of a revival of trade, I accepted his terms, which were house, firing,[5] and wages together, making up about eighteen shillings a week. Although provisions still ranged very high, I thought, if no worse luck broke in upon us, we might do tolerably well, as it would be a regular thing. So after a further trial of a month or so my master finding me tractable and always obedient (contrary to the manner of my predecessor who had been, as I heard, drunken and refractory), and having drilled me into some of his odd ways, seemed to like me very well. Nor did I dislike my master. This gentleman was a most curious character – an odd compound; hard to describe. With all respect to his memory, I will just say a few words about him. His personal appearance: he was aged; rather below the middle stature; bluff, corpulent, of Sir John Falstaff make, and of aldermanic gait; he walked with the air of a true Old English Gentleman, with his stout ivory topped and steel spiked cane. His dress one might have supposed to be of a cut of the fashion worn in the days of Sir John: his coat of greenwood hue, and the rest, as they were. He had a fine ruddy countenance; was sharp-sighted –quick in thought –hurried in speech – had a big voice, even to a roar when excited; he was a little witty; sometimes very irritable, petulant, and passionate, and again calm, affable, and jocular. He was also very knowing, in his way. He had been brought up in the old buckle school of Walsall,[6] a long way back in the last century. If taken altogether, my master might have been reckoned, in the days of Robin Hood and Little John, a very clever and learned man.[7]

It may not be amiss to relate, by way of anecdote, a few of my master's eccentric sayings and doings. His residence being but half a street's length from the coal wharfs, his habits of business were to visit me and the workmen about three times a day. The trade panic continuing down to the next year. Many of the large manufacturers and tradesmen had become insolvent in rapid succession. Those, usually our best customers, failing, were the cause of heavy losses to my master. Such things, together with the gloomy prospect, made him extremely irritable. Others, again, who were dishonest, would not pay though able. That class annoyed

5 That is to say, fuel.

6 A footnote in the original text reads as follows: 'The buckle trade was, formerly, the staple trade of the town.'

7 It has unfortunately proved impossible to identify Jackson's colourful employer. However, an 1818 directory lists Thomas Jackson as 'agent to Foster & Fyfield' a coal merchant's firm located at the 'Old wharf' on Park Street in Walsall. See W. Parson and T. Bradshaw, *Staffordshire General & Commercial Directory* (Manchester: J. Leigh, 1818), p. 316.

him very much: yes, and me, too, in having to dun them so often.[8] I could always tell when my master's temper had been ruffled by some of them. As he approached the office, in his blustering passion he would strike the pavement with his spike till it struck fire again, and talking loud to himself, as he rolled into the office, his utterance would be half choked with rage. He would say, "Thomas, how much does that rascal – (naming such an one) – owe me, and how long?" I would refer, and should perhaps find the debt to be £17. 15s., and owing fifteen months. "Now look you there, Thomas, I have just seen that fellow get into the coach, going to Birmingham, dressed like a gentleman, and he owes me all that money. Don't you think it's a shame, Thomas?" Of course I should answer in the affirmative. He would then observe, "When I was in the buckle trade, thirty-five years ago, I had to go to Birmingham, too, with my goods, but no coach for me, Thomas; no, no. My wallet on my back, Thomas, carried all my goods: and my expenses there and back again, was two-pence half-penny, for bread and cheese and beer, while his will at least cost him ten shillings of my money. Don't you think, Thomas, he ought to be made to pay?" I should then be sure to side with my master, as it was just. "Thomas, you shall take some of these accounts to the lawyer; I'll bear it no longer. I don't like law, but when I do begin – when I once enter the field – (then courageously striking his spike on the floor) – I never give up till I am downright beat." His pet would then be over.[9] He would afterwards sit down and tell me some old anecdote of his juvenile days, and finish up with a hearty laugh. Perhaps on the way home a poor man would ask him for a lump of coal. He would turn back and whisper to me, "Thomas, give him a small lump, or he will come in the night and steal a big one." Another time a poor man in the street would want to beg of him, when he would bring him to me – (now I had never before heard of my master's liberality until he told me himself) – and say, "Thomas, give this poor man a penny for me." He would then add – "I never make a practise of wearing money in my pockets, for if I do, be it as much as ever it will, I am sure to give it away." In another of his eccentric ways he made me feel rather queer. Speaking of a fresh man whom he had employed, he set me to look strictly after him. "Although, Thomas," said he, "he may be a very honest man; but I always look after an honest man as I do a thief." I stopped my pen to look him in the face. When he saw the remark had affected me, he stepped up to me, and knudging [sic] my elbow, laughingly said – "What do you think I do that for, Thomas?" I said, "I am at a loss to know, sir." "Why to keep him honest, to be sure, Thomas; that's my way." I could but smile at my master's simple, though rather piquant manner of keeping an honest man honest. These and such sort of ways and doings were always flowing from the odd compound in my master's budget.

8 Dun: to harass, pester or importune.

9 Pet: a fit of ill humour.

At time flew on from year to year, it was seldom that any year passed away without producing some extraordinary event for me. Towards the close of 1819, it was to be that I should have a happy increase of family, in the birth of a daughter. This event had nearly caused the death of my poor wife; but, however, after a long illness, she providentially recovered.[10]

But I must turn again to my good master for another word or two. Down to this period there was very little prosperity in the trades. My master's irritable temper was sometimes raised to a pitiable height of petulant frenzy, caused by the nonpayment of so many outstanding debts. After one of those distressing fits – it being then very wet weather, in the time of corn harvest – his temper settled down into a calm, sullen silence, and he sat him down, speechless, at the office fire, while I was quiet in my books. After some half hour's cogitation in his way, he turned suddenly round to me, and, in a lamentable strain – seeming to have emanated from the very climax of my master's logical genius – first deploring the bad harvest, and, as the farmers were our greatest customers with long credits, said, "Now, Thomas, the farmers are all ruined, I shall never get their money; the roguish part of the trades people will not pay me – there never can be any more good trade for honest men to pay me – trade and prosperity of this country has been up to its height – the nation is ruined. I have foreseen this would come to pass many years ago: building property is next to good for nothing: I always said it would be so. I took care never to build, and said those were fools that did. The funds, Thomas, the funds for me; I always said that would be the only safe property. Besides, Thomas, you see all things are being brought to a stand, and must go back. No improvements can take place; there will be no more inventions – all inventions have been that ever will be. The art of man is quite exhausted, therefore how is it possible for improvements to take place? So the best way would be, Thomas, for those who have got any money in trade to get it out as soon as they can, and go and live on it, or they'll lose it. England will now go back again to its origin, and be like unto some of the old ruined nations we read of." With these fearful bodings, and Lilliputian prognostics, would my poor master perplex himself day by day. Then, after a pause, he would say, "Now what do you think of all this, Thomas?" waiting for my opinion, though I did not often dissent lest I should offend him. But I could not help, in this instance, saying, "Well, sir, in giving my opinion, I must beg to deviate largely from yours on these important matters." "You do!", said he, sharply, and not allowing me to proceed further, continued: "You are too young, yet, in the world, Thomas, to form a right judgment on weighty things. By the time you have seen as many years as I have, you will see them as clear as I do now." So with his usual air of self-complacency, and striking his spike hard on the floor, [he] turned and left the office, not at all pleased. Besides these, other new perplexities sprung up for my master: as his

10 Maria Jackson was christened at St Matthew's Church, Walsall on 26 April 1820.

trade for many years past had been almost a monopoly, he had then to encounter a great opposition from a number of small beginners in the coal trade, who, by contriving to undersell, curtailed our orders still very much. Thus with the gloomy aspect of the times, and the long list of debts on the books, my master despaired of ever doing any more good in the coal trade; and at length, in the year 1821, resolved to relinquish it altogether. Then, thought I, here is another reverse about to take place in my wavering destiny—what new adversity am I to be driven into next? However, in this case, I was frightened before I was hurt. The parties to whom the trade was transferred thought, from my practise, knowing the customers so well, and having given satisfaction to my late employer for nearly four years, they could not do better than take me with the trade, as their clerk. So I then parted from my good old master, who was a downright worrit to all the rest of his servants, but never found fault with me.[11]

My new employers were a partnership, each taking an active part. One was an innkeeper of Walsall, a man of gentlemanly conduct and manners. The other was a surly ill-bred fellow – a totally unlettered ignoramus, whom I disliked very much, and not without cause, as he very soon became my enemy, and would have discharged me, but the innkeeper would not consent, he having found the bulk of the cash in the trade, and I being well known to him before, I was safe in his hand. Through my knowledge of the trade before, and my perseverance again, the business of the first year was very prosperous, netting a large profit, which so lifted up the head of my surly master, that he relaxed in his part, and tried to ape the gentleman. The alehouse then became his constant resort. Always drunk and domineering, he ordered me to quit his employ. When I told his partner, a quarrel ensued about me, and the innkeeper said he should be the first to quit. It was so. He would have ruined the innkeeper, as the ruffian set no bounds to his profligacy. The innkeeper resolved on a dissolution, and at the close of 1823, a valuation of all stock was taken, and I was ordered to balance the accounts between them, when, lo! poor silly Mr. Surly was found £130 indebted to the innkeeper, which was never paid. After having beggared his wife and a large family, he pined and died unlamented.[12]

In the year 1824 (another disastrous period) I was visited with a most distressing event; the worst of all, viz. the loss of my dear partner – the wife of my youth.[13] She having been bred in the milder air of London, and, withal, delicately constituted, the cold atmosphere of Staffordshire, threw her into consumption; having then shared with me, during twelve years, in all the trials and difficulties incident to our allotted station; and after suffering a long, lingering, and painful illness, was cut

11 Worrit: someone who pesters or worries unnecessarily.

12 Pined: languished, suffered a mental and physical decline.

13 Maria Jackson was probably the 'Mary Jackson', aged thirty-four at death, who was buried at St Matthew's Church in Walsall on 7 July 1824. See 'National Burial Index for England & Wales'.

off in the midway of life, at the age of thirty-four. This bereavement I looked upon as the greatest of all misfortunes, so far, through my eventful life, as it involved me in great trouble, more so than otherwise, owing to the loss of my limb, in doing a mother's part for two little children – a girl four, and a boy eight, years old. It grieved me for a long time; but it was fortunate for them that my employ was at home. Worst of all, I had no time but in the night to nurse them in their little illnesses. My love for the children was such, that I could not be satisfied with any old woman I employed to do for them, so I resolved to do all for them myself, except their washing and mending, and that I would sometimes do a little of in the night. With this painful difficulty I cheerfully struggled on for about two years, when, fortunately, my poor wife's brother, an eminent engraver in London,[14] but who was not before very friendly with me, having no children, sent for, and took away from me the little girl, and reared and educated her until she was twelve years old.[15] This was so great a kindness, that I thought my distant brother-in-law the best friend I ever had. The boy being now about ten years old became a little useful in going of errands, &c.

My best master having got rid of his ruinous partner, continued to carry on the trade, and I remained with him until the year 1828, when after his prosperous doings at innkeeping, he became above the black-ware merchandise,[16] and resolved to give it up altogether. He sold off the stock and let the trade into the hands of another. My new master (for I was again transferred with the trade) was a young man, a tradesman in the town, who had before been doing a little in the coal business, [and] was, seemingly, anxious to get me as his clerk, even at an advance of wages. That man, too, whose conduct towards me deserved the strongest reprehension, after having gained an interesting point, by employing me, most dishonourably broke his agreement; and at the end of three months discharged me faultless. However, in charity, I will not now spend my nutgall,[17] in writing him in its bitterness. The reader may think, by this time, I must have had some queer and extraordinary characters for my masters, to please and endure with, by the way of getting my living. How bitterly galling to the man of common sense and honest mind, who, of hard necessity, has to crouch to the insulting domination of an ignoramus, or the crafty knave; with what scorn does his wounded spirit rear its crest in execrable contempt, and turn and set its foot upon the neck of the petty tyrant!

14 A footnote in the original text identifies Jackson's brother-in-law as 'Mr. Hall, of Bury Street, Bloomsbury.'

15 Jackson's brother-in-law was Sidney Hall (c.1788/9?-1831), an accomplished London engraver and cartographer celebrated for his atlases and maps of the ancient world. Hall made generous provision in his will for his nieces and nephews, including Thomas Jackson's children Charles and Maria. See *ODNB* and TNA, PROB 11/1783/22.

16 That is to say, coal.

17 Nutgall: that is to say, ink.

I then became my own master again. Of course the sudden reverse put me about, but I consoled myself by considering how long I had been stationary, and without being routed by outrageous fortune that so usually waylaid me in my thorny path. I truly might congratulate myself on having remained in one situation for eleven years altogether. It might be supposed, in that long and regular employ, I ought to have saved a little money, but that was not to be; for such had been high price of all provisions, clothing, and other necessaries requisite for housekeeping; together with expenses incurred by the lingering and protracted illness of my poor wife, and what followed it, in having had to bury my poor father a fortnight after, I had to go and seek a fresh fortune with scarce a pound in my pocket. In this unlooked for dilemma I did not know what to do next; I could not meet with any other situation as a clerk, and the shop trades happened to be at that time very bad; I had no prospect there. After a few weeks' consideration, I thought would try a day and evening school. Having a large chamber in my house, I advertised myself to teach reading, writing, and arithmetic, at a cheap rate. This seemed in a few weeks to promise very fair, so that I had often as many boys as I could well manage, especially of that clownish and refractory description that my neighbourhood produced: surely, thought I, never had [a] schoolmaster such an awkward squad of juvenile clodpoles to teach as fell to my lot: I had read somewhere of the miseries of the schoolmaster, and certainly it was now my case; for I had to cultivate ignorance of the grossest kind, and stupidity in its natural state. Here was hob and clog – pitman and clayman – and all such kind of "stars of the earth." Some great brawny faced boys from the straw yard, with their little blue smockfrocks, stiffened with grease, and their hair, twisted in dirt, sticking out like bunches of radishes laid on their heads, and perhaps, interwoven with cow-hair, and with hobnailed shoes a pound weight each. Another class of miners' children would be clad in thick coarse velvet, made large enough for them to grow in for years; their trousers furled up six inches above the ankle; the coat tail down to their heels; shoes well hobnailed; and their hair resembling a furze bush, with, perhaps, some straw in it; all as ignorant as the young animals of the field; no kind of decency taught them at home, they were naturally hardened in impudence. I had often to fatigue myself with caning them; but the velvet squad bid me defiance. I might just as well flog the coat of the rhinoceros, to make him feel as them; so I had to make them strip; this was required before I could obtain any sort of order and obedience. Again, a mother would bring a fresh boy by the hand, and say, "Plase sur, yo munna gie this boy the stick; hey's a nice lad, hey'll do onythink yo tell'n him." "Very well, I shall try him," said I; when, perhaps, before the day was over, I have found him an incorrigible little ruffian; so I would send him back to his "ma," with my compliments, to educate her darling boy herself. Another "ma" would bring her offspring, and say, "Sur, this lad is such tygar, as I dunna kno' what to do with him. Yo mun gie him the cayen well and never mind how he cries." "I will try him," I would say; when I should find this child the very opposite of the other; of good intellect, docile, tractable, and pleased to be instructed. So much for mothers' judgment of their own children. To be sure my flock were not all of the wild sort; being mixed, I had some boys of respectable tradespeople, which of course were of a superior quality, and, therefore, less troublesome. Scarcely any of them were allowed remain long enough with me, to receive much profitable learning, or to do me any credit. Some few, of the brightest intellect, belonging to my cloudy constellation of dim stars, would, through my indefatigable pains, be able to read and right [sic] very well, and get through the first simple rules of arithmetic, by the end of six months. This was generally thought by the parents to be an accomplished education. The boys would then be removed from school and put to work, and in another six months, perhaps, forgot all they had learned. These, not forgetting the nonpayments, are but few of the miseries of the schoolmaster so situate[d], and which I had to endure. Now I must shut the school door for a moment, while I relate a circumstance of some importance, concerning my future welfare, as the saying is, "for the better or the worse."

This year had already produced an adverse incident, of no trifling disadvantage to me, in old Dame Fortune having found out my quiet means of getting my living. No thanks to her, I soon again jumped into other means, though somewhat of an irksome character, yet I had one consolation withal – I had neither the ignoramus, nor the crafty knave, to domineer over me. And, perhaps, after all, my removal from my former employ was, by the unseen working of the mysterious hand, to be ultimately for my good. However, to come to the important point, this year, though near its end, old Mr. December had, in his budget, an event extraordinary for me. And, as I have said before, what is to be will be – but that's not all about it; then I must tell all about it; and the truth is, without any further palaver, I got married to a second wife on Christmas Day.[18] It was so. Nobody blamed me for it; and, thank God, she is living while I write this narrative, in my sixty-second year. I had been then four years and a half a widower, without woman's help in my house, except an old one to clean once a week. Having got an appendage to my school business, as a collector of moneys for bankruptcies, insolvents' estates, and other things, all my leisure hours were occupied, so that I had no time to dress my meal; my house always dirty, and every thing in it going to wreck, I deemed most prudent the step I had taken, in marrying a respectable widow, who was near about my own age, and who had also seen and felt a share of the world's buffetings in her former sphere of life. What I could make by my commission as a money collector, and the produce of my fluctuating school, made us a tidy living.

18 No corresponding marriage record could be located; the pair probably wed at St. Paul's Chapel in Walsall, for which the relevant registers do not appear to have survived. However, according to the 1841 and 1851 censuses, Thomas Jackson's second wife was named Elizabeth and was born in Lichfield, Staffordshire circa 1789-90. See TNA, HO 107/983/14, Walsall returns, p.32 and HO 107/2061, St Matthew's Parish, Aston near Birmingham returns, p.8.

Things of this kind and manner went on pretty smooth for about two years, when, as though adverse fortune had not done me mischief enough before, to my great privation, a national school was opened on a large scale, and, being but a short distance from me, I very soon began to feel the effects of its working, so that the number of my motley pupils was continually on the decrease, until I had lost more than one half. This was a sad drawback, which I never after recovered. Although it still withered away to be not worth any man's attention, yet I was forced to submit to it, and consider it as part and parcel of the "crook in the lot" that was designed for us.

About this time, my son having turned fourteen, it was desirable he should be provided with a trade, about which I was very anxious, as it regarded his welfare for life. But at this time, too, the trades of the town were so bad, that masters were glad to give up rather than receive apprentices. Here I was in a great strait. I had even offered a premium of ten pounds with him to several trades, but [it was] not accepted because the masters had no employ for boys. At length I met with one which I was persuaded was a good chance for the boy. It was then a money-getting trade: fifteen pounds premium was demanded by the master, who was a gig horse collar-maker. This demand was a heavy blow to me, in my then diminishing means; however, I resolved at all sacrifice to give it. I did so, for the good of the boy; but the self-denial, in consequence, afterwards, was long and trying. Then I had again to plod my way through the maze of difficulty which lay before me. I had no longer hope of schoolkeeping keeping me at housekeeping. I then tried every means to obtain some sort of a situation as a clerk, by answering advertisements, or otherwise inquired for, but all to no purpose: every application failed, and often, as I thought, through my mutilated appearance; however that might be, I had to remain as I was until old Dame, or Miss Dame Fortune, should again, in their freaks, give me another twist, by laying in my path some new and hapless event. And, alas for me! my distrustful bodings at no distant period were to be realised.

I pass over a gloomy lapse into the year 1832. That memorable year. It is well remembered by me, for the sufferings I had to endure in the very heart of it. It will be remembered, too, by all, as a matter of history. I allude to the period when this country, and especially this district, was afflicted with that awful visitation [of] the Asiatic or spasmodic cholera.[19] The town and neighbourhood of Bilston were first attacked by the epidemic, in all its virulence, carrying off, at one deadly sweep, more than six hundred of the inhabitants, in less than three weeks; meanwhile it was also finding its way to Walsall; and, as was thought by the medical gentlemen,

19 Cholera arrived in Walsall at the beginning of August 1832; the town had 346 cases and 85 deaths. See William White, *History, Gazetteer and Directory of Staffordshire* (Sheffield: Robert Leader, 1834), p. 223 and Frederic W. Willmore, *A History of Walsall and Its Neighbourhood* (Walsall: W. Henry Robinson, 1887), p. 421.

by way of the canal, direct from Bilston. Their opinion seemed to be borne out by the facts that followed, leaving no doubt that the dire disease had been attracted by the water. The first victim that perished by it, in Walsall, was a man who lodged in a house on the bank of the canal terminus; he was well and dead in twenty-four hours. Another man working in a boat shared the same fate. The whole neighbourhood, that stood within the breeze of wind from this part of the canal, became immediately infected with the disease. My dwelling stood in the midst; and not more than forty yards from the water. I saw a young man at work on the canal side, who was there taken ill; he went home sick – took the disease with him – gave it [to his] wife – and in two days they died. The whole neighbourhood had it in their houses. From the sickening and agonizing pains in the stomach and bowels, with the torturing cramp in the limbs, life, in the strongest men, seldom held out more than thirty hours. So terrifying was the number of deaths, daily, that no one cared to put them into their coffins; neither could bearers be obtained, to carry the dead to be buried; so that a man was employed by the authorities, with an old hearse and one horse, to go round the neighbourhood, from house to house, twice a day, to carry off each corpse as soon as possible. The disease had been making havoc three or four days before it seized upon me. I was in hopes we should have escaped; but, no, it was written in the lot. My wife and I were sitting at breakfast with open doors, it being very hot, in the month (about the 4th) of August: I was suddenly seized with dimness of sight and giddiness in the head. It was the epidemic. I got up and staggered to the door for air, but was forced to hold myself by the wall. My wife, alarmed, advised me to try to go to the doctor who lived just below. With much difficulty I did stagger there: I found his surgery crammed full of applicants, craving help for their dying friends at home. He looked me in the face and saw what I wanted. He then made me drink a draught of about two ounces of something, bidding me go to bed immediately. I staggered home again; my wife got me to bed. On telling her of the draught, she became more alarmed, knowing that many around us who had had these draughts went to sleep under its potency, but never awoke again. I had to take my chance of that. The power of the medicine soon threw me into a lethargy or stupor; yet I had about me some sense of understanding. As I lay upon my back, my stomach and breast seemed ready to burst with fulness; heaving and falling at long intervals, similar to the stroke of immense bellows. In this state I lay in agonizing pain till afternoon. My finger and toe nails turned black as ink. The doctor had just got time to run up to see me. He had a peculiar method of treating his cholera patients, by which he saved many. It was by stripping the body, laying it naked on the floor, and dashing two or three buckets of cold water over it; then [he] put them to bed in the blankets, with medicine and so forth. He told my poor terrified wife he could not stay then, but she must prepare the required quantity of water, and he would return and apply it to me. She did so; but I was in such a state of stupefaction, that I was altogether unconscious of it being brought into the chamber. By four in the afternoon another doctor had looked in, for all the doctors of the town were then employed in our distressed neighbourhood. He did not see me, that I know of, but he found my wife had taken the epidemic; he gave her something out of his pocket to take, and I left her. She came to my bed and shook me, with hopes to make me understand that she had got the water for me to be soused with, and how she felt herself. I did at last understand; and perceived she had taken the disease.

Having confidence in the water application, and being alarmed for the safety of my wife, I roused from my lethargy, and a sort of wild desperate courage came over me. I leaped from my bed: no doctor at hand, I made my poor trembling wife strip for her life, and I poured that water over her which she had prepared for me. Oh! it was a distressing scene. I then got her into bed with me; there we lay, writhing in all the agonies of the disease, looking for death every hour. My little daughter, about twelve years old, was then at home from London; but, poor thing! she was so terrified that she could render us no assistance. No neighbour dared to come in to do any thing for us. My doctor had, in the afternoon, left medicine, at my bedside, to be applied every two hours; but we had not sense enough to take it, or even strength to reach it. The house door being open all night, my doctor, with a physician, at midnight, came into our chamber. I had just got up to give my wife some medicine; when he said he was then come to apply the water to me, as he had no time to come before. I told him my wife had taken the disease just as I had; and I had myself applied it to her. The two medicals looked astonished at each other, the physician tapping me on the back, said, "Well done, well done; you have saved your wife, and think we can save you now, without the water." This dreadful night passed as it had begun with us. Next morning my little daughter was very unwell; I feared she had taken the epidemic. I bid her go to the doctor for some medicine, and then run away to a farm house outside the town, where I had some friendly acquaintance; she did, and remained there several weeks. This thought, in the trying moment, perhaps saved her life. In our helpless state we lay, without any other help but our medicine, until night again, when our doctor came to examine us, and said he observed a sort of fever in our case, which, in some measure, would counteract the virulence of the cholera, and we should, he had no doubt, get over it. This, of course, was cheering information; still I feared much for my poor wife, as she had never ceased vomiting from the first hour she was taken. The weather, distressingly hot and sultry, was, too, all against us. About the middle of the second night, I put on all my vigour to go down and try to make a cup of coffee for us; after great difficulty I succeeded. It was a happy thing for my wife, as it tended to allay her vomiting; but no particle of food did we take for three days, but drank coffee. Still in our chamber, lying in our sad condition, and through not being seen by the neighbours, we were, by their surmise, reported all over the town to be dead. As soon as we were able to look out of the chamber windows to the street, we saw the vehicle of the dead, continuing to patrol the neighbourhood, to carry away the new victims of the awful and terrifying pestilence. We remained in our feeble and exhausted condition, confined to our bed, six or seven days. The doctor would see us once a day: no one else. No friend dared yet venture in, even to ask how we were. Soon after, however, my wife began rapidly to recover, and, as the doctor said, through me having poured the water over her, so that she was able to render me some help; and, by the end of about six weeks, she got quite well. But not so with me; I had not got over mine by the end of six months, so tenacious and lingering was the debility left by the disease. After we were able to leave our chamber, and to be seen at the street door, people passing by, seeing our altered appearance, and having heard of our death, would stop amazed, and, gazing upon us, could not believe their eyes, as to whether we were really the persons they had known before. And, also, when I came to walk in the streets of the town, I was pointed and gazed at just as one might have been who had risen from the dead.

This awful dispensation of Providence, was by this time (after its virulence had subsided, and which lasted about fifteen days) looked upon as a warning scourge, from the anger of God, for the wickedness of our nation. I, one of the chastened survivors, permitted to tell the tale of woe, have much, very much, to be thankful for, that I did, in that distressing instance, too, escape from the jaws of death. But it was, besides my long suffering, a woful [sic] stroke to me, in deranging all my little affairs depending on our welfare. As it not only swept away my little flock of schoolboys, but also, through inability, caused me to lose some of my engagements as a money collector. In this new dilemma, I did not know what to do next; I was often at my wits end, while my health and strength were so much impaired, as not to be able to work at anything. Time passing on, in this gloomy state of things with me, brought us into the year 1833, and by the spring I had perfectly recovered my health and strength. During my vacation behind, I had been resolving and re-resolving, about turning my hand again to my former trade of plating. After having been away from it fifteen years, it was a staggering thought how I should remember it again. However, being driven, as it were, into a corner by my late adversity, I saw no alternative, but try I must. But how to begin was the next question. I knew I could not work well enough to go into a shop as a journeyman, nor was it then likely I could make goods perfect enough to sell; so there I was still in a strait. At last I resolved to get some tools and materials to work upon, convert my schoolroom into a workshop, and there practise myself until I could manufacture goods that would sell, and bear a competition with others in the trade. I did so for many weeks, until I had satisfied myself as to the quality being sufficient. I then went to the saddlers' ironmongers, who dealt in such things, and, to my great joy, succeeded in opening a connection with one worthy gentleman, and, some while after, with another. So that having the cheering prospect before me of getting plenty of work, as a manufacturer on my own account, with my health perfectly established, my courage once more raised up again; and finding I could get a decent living, and still be my own master, I bid adieu to quill-driving, finding more pleasure, as well as more profit, in driving the burnisher. I then determined to devote all my energies to the prosecution of my trade, and took another house, with a proper workshop, where I could fix up my apparatus to better advantage. I looked upon that period as being, perhaps, the only opportunity that might ever be given to me of trying to lay up a few pounds for old age and infirmity, if should live to need it.

My wife, encouraged by the prudent thought, and being healthy and active, resolved to render me every assistance in her power, between leisure intervals in her domestic affairs. That was as it should be; it was like pulling together in the same draught; and, as I said then, the benefit would be found at some future time; perhaps in a day of need. Many wives have I known who have scornfully refused to soil their hands, or otherwise take a part in a small business of their husband's, in the days of health and strength. When old age and infirmities have overtaken them, instead of pouting, and living luxuriantly, [they] have been humbled by pinching poverty, and crouched to the meanness of living upon the labour of others. There being some parts in my work, not to be reckoned labour, which a woman could do very well, after a little instruction my wife became very useful, and a good help. We next resolved to stick close to the shop, all the year round; make no holidays; see no costly society; have no expensive acquaintance; and deny ourselves all manner of pleasures that would cost either money or time. The very low price of my goods at that time would not allow of any such indulgences, so that no time must be lost. As I was not able to do, through the loss of my limb, as much work in the day as another man would who was not logged with a Chelsea "slow-time traveller," I used to make out by working extra hours. I resolved, too, that I would not extend my trade so as to employ either journeyman or apprentice, as I had no wish to eat the bread earned by any other hands than my own. My habits of labour were usually from five in the morning until eight at night, mostly the year round, and with that I was content and happy; my partner of industry was happy, too. Having no incumbrance, my daughter having got a good service, which was also a desirable instance; my wife always willing to work at any thing she could do to forward me in getting a shilling, with our unremitting labour, and close attention to business, together with a strict economy and prudence, I had, by the end of the first year, contrived to save about twenty pounds. This being placed quietly in the savings' bank, served as a stimulus to our future exertions to increase the stock.[20]

With a continuance of this kind of rigorous proceeding, in the close application to work and self-denial, we had, by the end of the second year, saved about half as much more as in the first. This great prosperity, for so I had reason to call it, as nothing of so favourable a character had ever before fallen into my lot, and which, when comparing the prospect with the retrospect, was cheering indeed. But with all that encouraging view before me, I did not expect to find golden crows in my beaten down trade. I knew very well that if I got any gold at all out of it, it must be in exchange for the toil of my body, and the sweat of my brow. The strength and power of body being of course diminished, in consequence of the

20 Jackson is listed in an 1834 directory as a plater and buckle maker living in Nickol's Court, Stafford Street in Walsall. See White, *History, Gazetteer and Directory of Staffordshire*, p. 443.

missing limb, my ordinary exertions forced upon me copious perspirations, to the great prejudice of my health; besides, my time in life, then more than fifty years old, it was getting a day too late to make continual, long, and toilsome labour days. However, although cheerfully proceeding, without a murmur, yet I could not help thinking of the curse pronounced in the fatal garden of Eden, when the Lord said, "In the sweat of thy face shalt thou eat bread." And I, being a son of Adam's taint, it was truly verified in me. Well, with all this, and more, without pining, "Forward" was the inspiring watchword, but still with caution, lest I should fall into laxity and self [con]gratulation in my little ray of sunshine. I had not forgotten the thorny path which brought me, at last, to this quiet station. I remembered the savage pranks of outrageous fortune, and the crooked windings in my mysterious destiny. All these things I remembered too well, to be lulled into thoughtless security, but kept watch, like the sentinel near the enemy's outpost, expecting to be surprised by something new, of an adverse character. After three smooth years had passed away, uninterrupted by any extraordinary or alarming event, and nothing worse befalling us than a little ordinary sickness, or the like, it seemed as though the mysterious hand (as I have often called it) of Divine Providence was about working some change in my destiny of a more favourable nature, tending to my comfort in the winter of life. With these encouraging ideas, I joyfully hoped in it, trusted in it, and prayed for it. Both myself and wife were then in tolerable good health, to proceed with our firm resolutions in sticking to business, prudence, and economy, and so winding up another good year's account, to be carried, as before, to interest. Trade then becoming very bad, was, of course, a serious check to my little gatherings; but, fortunately, provisions were comparatively lower than ever I had known them before. Four pounds and a half of bread for sixpence, and joints of good mutton at fourpence-half-penny per pound. But these happy times for the poor man were but of short duration; a reaction taking place in the provision trade, up again it went: but not so with the price of labour. However, I went on in my humble perseverance in abstinence and self-denial, prudently making the best of every thing in my way, with smiling Providence to cheer my best endeavours; and having met with no untoward event, of adverse character, in my progress through seven or eight years together, I reckoned that portion of my life, although the hardest laboured portion, to be the most prosperous and tranquil period I had ever enjoyed from my youth up.

In the year 1840, I summed up the fruits of my diligent labours, through my arduous course, when I found, to my great joy, about one hundred and seventy pounds in my bank book. This was a glorious summing up; a large sum, I thought, for me to possess after all my misfortunes. A wonderful change of fortune: the reverse of the evil I had before experienced: especially so when I looked back and saw myself lying on my bed, bleeding and freezing, in the horrid prison of Bergen-op-Zoom. Could I then have dreamed of ever seeing in my life such a day of change as this? From the brink of despair to the summit of joy and peace – the thought is sacred! It is wonderful to me that, after that sad disastrous affair, and its dire train of adversities, and sufferings in consequence, that I am living and doing well, thirty-two years after. It is to me a miracle. A moment's solemn reflection assures me to Whom I am indebted for what I am, and Whom I can never repay with thanksgiving, when I remember how often His wonderfully mysterious hand snatched me from the jaws of death. Twice He rescued me from a watery grave in the perilous deep: again, preserved me in the imminent deadly battle: next, delivered me out of prison, while yet bleeding, in the hands of a rapacious enemy: and, again, when at the sepulchre door, brought down through intense suffering, in healing my wounds: and, lastly, when life was despaired of in the awful visitation of cholera. Then, after all these merciful preservations in so many instances of peril, He has, in furtherance of His bountiful goodness, been pleased at length to raise me up, so far, to enjoy the common comforts of life in my advanced aged. These many instances of His providential goodness often constrain me to say with the psalmist, "What shall I render unto the Lord for all His benefits towards me?" Alas! what have I to render? All I have is His already; given unto me in trust, and, therefore, is His own; so that, rightly considered, I have nothing of my own to render, but my poor, feeble, worthless thanks. These will I cheerfully give; in the words next spoken by the psalmist, "I will take the cup of salvation and call upon the name of the Lord." With such peaceful reflections I, amidst my toiling days, enjoyed a tranquility of mind known only to contentedness, after being taught in the school of adversity.

I next began to think of making some better profit of my little fund than the produce of bank interest. After a consultation with my wife, I resolved to build a little house, to cover our grey heads with, if we should live to occupy it. Accordingly I bought a piece of freehold land, in an airy situation, outside of the town of Walsall, and had a house and workshop, with outhouses, wall fencing to retired yard, &c., built and finished in July, 1840. As soon as it was fit for occupation, we went to enjoy it and there carried on my little trade in my own workshop. The first cost of the building, including the land and all other things, amounted to £175, a greater sum than I intended to lay out, but the builder, a knavish fellow, in his crafty manner, beguiled me into further cost. This lavish outlay, as I thought it, devoured all my little fund, so that I had to begin again, with renewed resolutions, to work for more. Encouraged by the past, I cheerfully went on with new ardour, still continuing my former habits of perseverance.[21] But after a short time I began to feel a withering slackness in trade; that having a serious continuance, my progress in well doing became very much impeded, and, therefore, all did not go on so well. After having lived in my own domicile about a year and half, I found an inconvenience in being

21 Thomas Jackson, then aged 56, and his wife Elizabeth, aged 52, were both living in their newly-built house in John Street, Walsall for the 1841 census. Jackson was listed as a plater by trade. See TNA, HO 107/983/14, Walsall returns, p. 32.

too far from my trade connections, and having an opportunity of letting my premises to a good tenant, I did so, at a rent of £10 a year.[22] I then went to a more convenient situation in the town. In this fresh residence I continued my exertions in the usual manner, but with varied success, trade being held much in check under the influence of different gusts of political excitement, so that a panic almost prevailed, which was of course very hurtful to me. But what was more to be deplored, my health, which had borne me up in my shop labours for nine years, now began to give way; not so much through the infirmities of age, as the sharp discipline I had imposed upon myself, in the close confinement to my business. What was worse, and the most probable, were the injurious effects received from frequently inhaling the hot and burning fumes of pernicious ingredients which I necessarily had to make use of in my work. These injurious effects wrought upon my constitution such debility as to often bring me under medical treatment. My complaint was chiefly extreme pain in the breast and throat; a disease which my doctor called bronchitis, occasioned by inhaling pernicious vapours as I have before stated. But this was not all my suffering from the same cause. It brought upon me that miserable malady called nervousness; a malady that renders life half a death, as it drags along in dreary melancholy. These two complaints are said to be incurable, and so far, after seven years' experience, I have too much reason to believe the assertion.

The failing of my health was a sad misfortune; the complicated disorder producing such great lassitude and waste of bodily strength, as frequently to disable me from carrying on my work. In those grievous cases I was forced to pay for work, though badly done, to keep my little trade together. Such things continuing were very distressing; especially so, as I found, by long application, the malady did not yield to the power of medicine, only as a temporary relief. I became alarmed about carrying on my business. However, I continued to work, at intervals, with all the power I had, which soon again brought me under medical care. After more than two years of this suffering in anxiety, and no permanent relief apparent, all hopes of further prosperity in my trade vanished, and no more prospect of realizing a little surplus at the year's end – after a few more months, in my feeble efforts to carry on the business, my doctor advised me to give up the trade altogether, or it would assuredly be fatal to me. This was disheartening indeed. After hesitating, and trying again, and in hope, again, I found it a useless struggle: so with that sort of reluctance as the vanquished British soldier lays down his arms to the enemy, did I lay down my tools, in July, 1845, to my invincible enemy, disease. A new misfortune in my latter day, although a most untoward event, and likely to continue through life. I dared not murmur, knowing, as it is written, "The

22 An 1845 tithe map apportionment schedule shows that Jackson's property in John Street was rented to Thomas Hughes. See French, *Thomas Jackson*, p. 26. The site is currently occupied by Moldwel Products Ltd., a plastic injection moulding company.

Lord gave, and the Lord taketh away." I then, with humble resignation, began to consider the best means of disposing of my trade and its effects.

In a short time after, I had the opportunity of making such disposal, at a lamentable sacrifice, but that, under such circumstances, was unavoidable. After having made the best I could of all my stock in trade, and other effects thereunto belonging, I then, still to economise, moved into another house, a quiet place, at a less rent, being only five pounds a year. Being freed from all sorts of labour and business perplexities, and having the means of often walking out, I had every hope, with the aid of medicine, of improving, if not reinstating my health. More than six months, in lingering hope, had passed away, which brought me no real amendment; I had flattering intervals of improvement, but they were transient and delusive.

About this time, my tenant having quitted the house, and it being a more airy situation, I resolved to go and occupy it again. I did so. New hopes revived of deriving benefit from this change, that I might there again be able to enjoy my own workshop. But, alas! for me, after six months' residence there, too, and a long and beautiful summer had passed away, without finding any material amendment, I began to fall into despair. Sickened of medicine, and tired of blistering, bleeding, and plastering, I went to a skilful doctor for a thorough examination, when, to my sad dismay, he pronounced my constitution to be so much impaired, as not only to be unfit for work, but that I never should be able to do any kind of work. This was a woful [sic] stroke to my nervous system; it preying on my mind, made me worse than ever; and as I had, notwithstanding my loss of limb, been so many years inured to a diligent, active life, I then dreaded the prospect of passing the remnant of my days in idly nursing the gloomy melancholy of my deep-rooted malady, without hope of restoration. The cowardly nervous mind, incubus like, is constantly brooding o'er dismal things, and ruminating on fearful, visionary bodings, such as poverty, misery, and death, with a thousand other illusive thoughts, calculated to still depress the drooping spirit. I would often try to rally, with all the courage I had, from the lethargic gloom that oppressed my spirit, and the lassitude which enfeebled my frame, but in vain. Resigned to the will of Him who had ruled my destiny throughout, I then bowed to the mysterious hand that wields the chastening rod, and leaning only upon the hope of consolation from the same source, trusting that, if I should live a few more years in continuance of the debilitating malady, and thereby falling into poverty, the same mysterious hand which "feeds the ravens,"[23] would also provide for me. With these, and other such comforting thoughts, I endeavoured to cheer myself along my gloomy way.

It was a most happy circumstance for me that my good, industrious wife, was living, and enjoying the fulness of health. She who has shared with me in all my

23 Luke 12:24. This Biblical passage cautions against losing sight of God's teachings due to earthly worries or greed, proclaiming that the Lord provides for the material needs of all His creatures, even ravens. By citing this passage, Jackson expresses faith that God will protect him from want.

labours, prosperous or adverse, trials and troubles, through eighteen years, is yet spared, to render, by her willing hand, all she can towards the lessening of my sufferings; and is, also, always ready to join with me, in giving thanks to God, for all his mercies to us, and for what we are now, while lingering out a few more peaceful days under our own hard-earned roof, and living, in stinted frugality, on my national shilling per day, aided by the little residue of our provident self-denials. Under this roof I have written the narrative of my eventful life, in 1846, the sixty-second year of my age, at a labour occupying several months; while, for the most part of that time, under the pressure of much nervous, and other bodily debility. The object of my desire has been to leave a record of my history to my children, and their descendants, as a remembrance of some of their ancestry, at least as far back as my day. My narrative is a painful tale to be sure, in the main, especially the latter part of my military life; yet that may, nevertheless, be interesting, describing, as it does, the horrors of war, and its lamentable results.

When reviewing the numerous and varied scenes and changes in my rugged life, and tracing the mazy windings of my crooked path – observing the opposing incidents strewed in the way – marking scenes and circumstances, pleasing or painful, as they turned up – ranging the whole into a general summary of fortunate and unfortunate, it is seen that the unfortunate have been lamentably predominant; and when read by some of my descendants yet afar off, they may, perhaps, with a commiserating sigh, remark, "Truly our sire of old was a child of misfortune; though, withal, he manfully braved the storm of life with heroic fortitude and courage, worthy the character of a British soldier and a citizen."

Now, in conclusion, just before my narrative goes to press (May, 1847), I have yet one other extraordinary event to relate, but of a most happy import. During the present spring it has pleased God to restore my health to such a degree as I have not known for several years before. Thanks and praise be unto Him for ever! And, again, as my varying scenes and changes are only to end with my life, I have sold my little freehold, and left my native place to reside in Birmingham, to spend my latter days in the enjoyment of the society of my children and relations, who are settled there.

END OF NARRATIVE.

Appendix

My reason for making an appendix of this part of my narrative was, that, it describing a particular vein in my history, of serious import, I thought it best set apart and excluded from the grosser matter contained in my heterogenous miscellany. It is what I have not before explicitly narrated, and, being of sacred character, it may be read apart with more interest, if not instruction, than being interwoven with the period of my sad experience – I mean the important subject of religion. I wish to shew how, in my younger days, I had been led into the perilous errors of infidelity, by reading the works of anti-christian authors; the effects produced on my subsequent life, and my redemption from their thrall, in a singular manner, many years after. I was brought up, as a boy, to the Church of England creed, by my parents, though not with that strict superintendence I might have been. Therefore, that was as seed sown to the wind. Next, after that period, passing through twelve years of military life, where, at that time, so little was cared about the soul of the soldier, no encouraging stimulus [was] given to the young or ignorant, beyond the usual short Sunday morning service; so that this, too, was liable to be carried away by any novel or vain doctrine falling in the way. I was fond of going into churches when on a march, but this was out of mere curiosity. I used to buy books, but not religious ones. I would also borrow, greedily devouring any subject coming to hand. All this, of course, was stuffing the mind with perishable meat, and driving out every serious thought. Besides the trash read occasionally in the barrack-room, the guard-room, or camp, to wile away a dull or lazy hour, it was not unusual for works of immoral tendency, as well as anti-christian, to find their way into those places. Such as Paine's "Age of Reason," and his "Rights of Man,"[1] cleverly written things to be sure, in their way, well calculated to entrap the youthful and unwary

1 *Rights of Man* (1791) and *The Age of Reason* (1793-4) were both written by Anglo-American political activist and author Thomas Paine (1737-1809), today most famous for *Common Sense*, his 1776 pamphlet promoting American independence. In the two-part *Rights of Man*, Paine defended the French Revolution and criticized the British state and aristocracy as self-interested and oppressive. The three-part *Age of Reason* argued for deism and denounced Christian churches as corrupt. Though popular, both works were extremely controversial; Paine was convicted *in absentia* of seditious libel against the Crown for *Rights of Man*. Jackson's discussion of these works sheds intriguing light on the reading material perused by Napoleonic-era British soldiers.

reader. The "Rights of Man," being made up of outrageously enthusiastic politics, chiefly directed against all forms of kingly government, advocating democratical republicanism. The "Age of Reason", of still more pernicious tendency, goes to subvert the Christian faith, and destroy every vestige of that, the only true religion. It was that deadly poison that first took hold of my youthful mind, while in the army, and, in its malignant operation, turned into ridicule all that is written in the sacred book about the Saviour; so, becoming an infidel with the author, I must then join with him in the impious cry of "Priestcraft." But, though an infidel as to the Saviour, I could not be deceived as to the existence of a supreme God, and whom I always thought of with reverential awe. So that my religion could only then, at the best, if any at all, be called Deism, but which, under the Christian dispensation, is not acceptable with God. A truly awful condition! In this cloud of ignorance I still remained, long after I had left the army, so potent had been the poison to do its work. And at home, I found the dissemination of anti-christian works, among the working class, common as novels, and read with avidity. Not only Paine's, but many others, such as Volney's "Survey of the Ruins of Empires," Voltaire's "Palmer's Principles of Nature,"[2] &c. Having a knotty acquaintance with men of little learning, like myself, they having read and imbibed the same infidel principles, it was then unlikely I should be freed from the trammels of infidelity. In this perilous state I continued for some years longer, regardless of any form of worship, spending the Sabbath any way but the right, and perhaps in reading Volney's *Soul Ruining* "Ruins." This, both republican and anti-christian work, was so fascinating as to quite establish the infidelity I had imbibed of Paine.

Of the little I now remember of Volney: – he was a Frenchman;[3] he travels; arrives at the once magnificent, splendid, and opulent city of Athens, now in ruins. Struck with the exquisite beauty of some of the architecture, yet visible in the devastation, in one of his solitary perambulations by moonlight, he visits the ruins of a noble edifice, once a public building, or palace. Fascinated with the grandeur of the dilapidation, he falls into a deep reverie, and sitting down upon a fragment of one of the noble columns, once a proud supporter of the ancient pile, desolate[d] by war, he ruminates on the primary causes of such savage devastations as those before him, but in which he is perplexed and bewildered. A genii [sic] then appears to him, and offers to relieve his perplexity, by explaining to him the real and primary causes of such ruins – the effect of wars caused by religion. The genii then takes him up into the air, and shews him all the nations of the world, one after another, drawn out in separate groups, explaining to him their

2 *The Principles of Nature*, first published in 1801, was penned by American deist Elihu Palmer (1764-1806). Why Voltaire is mentioned as the author here is unclear. This probably reflects an error on the part of either Jackson or the printer as the French philosopher wrote no such work.

3 Constantin François de Chassebœuf, comte de Volney (1757-1820) was a French philosopher and historian. His pro-revolutionary *Ruins, or, Meditation on the Revolutions of Empires* (1791) denounced the influence of religion and called for the absolute separation of church and state.

creed, their tenets, and persecutions for religion. No two of them alike: the nations are ever at enmity; giving him the history of their rise and mutations; their wars and tumults; the depopulation and destruction of cities; the ruins of kingdoms and empires; with all the miseries that befal [sic] the human race; all of which he attributes to the conflicting creeds of their religions, as being the sole cause of the desolating wars. It might be readily expected that a work written in style so much like the Arabian Nights' Entertainments, would have an enchanting effect on the mind of the unwary. Yet the man of thought would soon see the inconsistency of Volney, in making religion, though the most peaceable sentiment that reigns in the heart of man, to be the primary cause of devastating war, and ruin of empires.

I had continued in the infidel principles for about fifteen years, up to the age of about forty, a time in life for a man to think, if ever he will think, seriously. I then began to examine those opinions in stronger thought. I got into a wavering condition. I would look into the Bible, but that was so very opposite to my infidel creed that I could not bear it. My wavering continued. I spoke of it to some of my blind acquaintance; it only served to bring upon me their ridicule and contempt. I became uneasy. I had seen some words in the book, saying, "Come out from among them." I pondered over these things with much concern. It so happened, at that time, I was the secretary to a benefit society in the town. The business over, I was returning home, about eleven o'clock, one moonlight night; for the nearest way, I took a solitary bye road, and near to it a new chapel was being built; its walls were only then reared a little above the ground. In passing, I stopped a moment to look on it. Being uninterrupted in my thoughts, something induced me to sit down upon a piece of timber, and looking on the work intended for a house of worship, I fell into a deep and serious meditation, thinking, if Paine and Volney were right, why are these men such fools as to lay out large sums on such follies? Why not pull down, instead of building new ones? But knowing, as I did, the projectors and supporters of the work, all of them men of high respect, and of much better learning than I had, can they, thought I, all be mistaken? Besides, hundreds more of their equals in the town, all of whom are worshippers of Jesus; can these, too, be all deluded by priestcraft, as Paine calls it, and I only, and some dozen others of my infidel acquaintance, be right, because we have adopted the opinions of Volney and Paine, which are altogether anti-christian? I was here staggered, and said, surely these men of better sense must be in the right way, and I have been cajoled and deluded. After a further debate with myself, I there and then resolved that, if I lived to see that house opened for divine worship, I would go, and take my place as a worshipper of God, and give up the "Age of Reason," and make a better use of my own reason. And so it came to pass.

When the chapel was finished, I engaged a gallery pew, and was present at the consecration and dedication to St. Paul.[4] But all that solemn ordinance was

4 St Paul's Chapel in Walsall was consecrated by the Bishop of Lichfield on 26 September 1826. See Willmore, *History of Walsall and Its Neighbourhood*, p. 401.

then to me a mere matter of curiosity. However, I resolved to attend the sabbath service in a regular way, and also to take my two little motherless children by the hand, to lead them in the way they should go thereafter. I felt myself very awkward in a congregation of regular worshippers, and, of course, very ignorant. My deep-rooted prejudices were not yet quite abandoned; my reverential awe and fear of God was unshaken, but I could not do reverence to that holy name of Jesus. No; my then half infidel neck would not bow to the name of the King of Glory; nor would I join in singing the appointed hymns, although I opened the book. The first sermon I heard I thought was very pointed towards me, and I did not at all like the minister's discourse; his name was Rogers;[5] and, being offended, I was thinking of not going any more. However, after an inward struggle during the week, I resolved to go again, thinking the offence might be only fancied. I went, and the same minister preaching, he seemed to keep his eye particularly on me, and spoke more pointedly than before, until I thought of going out of the chapel, so offensively was his discourse directed to me, just as though he had known my ways, and had made the sermon on purpose for me, he then being a stranger in the town. I then firmly thought, after this second offence, I could not endure to go again, and was in great confusion of mind all the ensuing week; but, by the next Sabbath, some overruling power had softened by stubborn temper, so that I again resolved, though with some reluctance, to try once more, and that should be finally to decide.

My infidel companions (men mostly in better circumstances in life than myself, and all of them of common respect, honest, upright, sober, just; unimpeachable in character, and always willing to do good; without a stain, except the serious blot called infidelity), had by that time became [sic] acquainted with my departure from their creed, consequently I had to bear the reproaching sting of the vituperance. This, of course, was a severe trial, to think that I might lose all my long-loved friends at once, by my act of recantation. However, the die was cast, and I could not go back. I went again to chapel, though, as I have said with some reluctance. I passed lightly through the service to the hymn usually sung before the Communion: I found the hymn, and then, as a matter of form, sung out with the rest. Coming to a strikingly touching passage, relating to God having so loved the world, as to give his only begotten Son Jesus Christ, to be a sacrifice for the sins of the whole world,[6] and the inconceivable love of the Son, in suffering death upon the cross for man's redemption, absorbed with the impressive thought, and feeling a sad conviction within, a mysterious thrill of gratitude rushed through my mind, which soon found its way to the eye, and I then let fall the first big tear, as a tributary offering to the dying love of my long rejected Saviour. Feeling ashamed, and

5 Reverend Thomas Rogers. See *The British Magazine and Monthly Register of Religious and Ecclesiastical Information...* (London: Rivington, 1837), vol. 11, p. 718.

6 The hymn was evidently based on John 3:16 – 'For God so loved the world, that he gave his only begotten Son, that whosoever believeth in him should not perish, but have everlasting life.' (King James Version)

thinking every eye was then upon me, I wanted a place wherein to hide my head. The minister, in his sermon, still spoke, as I thought, somewhat personal towards me, in strong terms of rebuking admonition, but which I received this time in a spirit of humility and mortification. I left the service with less confusion of mind than before, but still with deep concern at what had passed. At the evening service, another minister preached (a Mr. Cowley).[7] He was an aged gentleman, whom I had not heard before. He, too, I thought, seemed to particularly notice me; but in his very comforting sermon I thought it most singular, as though he had been told, that he should so pointedly mention about my tears in the morning; and, in a beautiful comforting manner, shewed me the cause producing those effects, saying it was the power of God working conviction, by the operation of his Holy Spirit, upon the obdurate and guilty heart of the awaking sinner. As I could not before understand these mysterious things, I received the comforting words with unbounded joy and gratitude. From that time forward, many were the briny drops that fell in the bitter cup of repentance, hoping they might one day find acceptance with Him whom I had so long persecuted. These things, of necessity, brought me into much tribulation, which "working patience, and patience hope," I became encouraged.

I then took to study the very book I had so long and so blindly rejected and despised—my Bible, in which I ever afterwards found a comforting treasure of incalculable worth. The Bible becoming "The chief stone of the corner,"[8] I cast from me all my other books as perishable trash; and in my debates with my former acquaintance[s], I used to maintain that the contents of all other books were lies, compared with its truths. I could see then I should be obliged to give up all my old companions; but the thought was still grievous to me, as I could see no fault in them except their infidelity. However, this was determined shortly after by another singular event. The wide spread of infidelity at that time, brought all the opposing powers of the pulpit into action. My minister, a very learned man, in a powerful address to his congregation, denounced infidelity as the worst of soul-destroying evils, to which I listened with the greatest attention. He shewed me the imminent danger I was escaping from—the loss of eternal life; and as though he knew my case with regard to my companions, had taken his text from that most appropriate portion of St. Paul's second epistle to the Corinthians, the 6th chapter, and from the 14th to the 18th verse, commencing "Be ye not unequally yoked together with unbelievers," and coming to the words in the 17th verse, with a strong emphasis read, "Wherefore, come out from among them, and be ye separate, saith the Lord, and touch not the unclean thing, and I will receive you." Again, in the 18th verse, "And I will be a father unto you, and ye shall be my sons and daughters saith the

7 Probably Reverend William Cowley (1773-1842). See Rupert Simms (ed.), *Bibliotheca Staffordiensis* (Lichfield: Lomax, the Johnson's Head, 1894), p. 123.

8 Psalm 118:22.

Lord Almighty!" With these emphatic and all absorbing words, I became deeply affected, and pondering them in my heart, instantly saw that there was no alternative, but the command of God, to "Come out from among them," must be obeyed, and that, however dear my infidel companions otherwise were to me, they must be given up. So after considering the encouraging and gracious promise which follows, "And I will receive you, and be a father unto you," I could not hesitate for a moment, but there and then, before I left the chapel, resolved in my heart to relinquish all my old and dear friends in error, and mentally said, with another portion of scripture, "Away from me, all ye workers of iniquity."[9]

After proceeding for awhile, altered as I then was, and in my new state of mind, I found more real happiness than I ever knew before, and have since the extraordinary change, up to this date, through two-and-twenty years, rejoiced with thanksgiving, in the hope that I have been one, "As a brand plucked from the burning."[10] Then having taken up the cross, and the pilgrim's staff, wherewith cheerfully, by God's help, to follow my gracious Saviour, as St. Paul observes, "Through evil report and through good report,"[11] and the rest of incidental buffetings of the enemy by the way, like Bunyan's pilgrim when leaving the city of destruction, and plodding his weary journey of hope to the celestial city.[12] The scales having fell from my eyes, I looked back, with a new vision, horror struck, upon the deceitful path I had so long walked in before my happy conversion. My escape from the thraldom of infidelity, was of course not of my own will. I have always looked upon it as a miraculous interposition of the power of God, that I might, if I would, upon true repentance, still receive salvation unto eternal life. I have written thus much to shew and prove the danger there is in reading the pernicious works of infidel or anti-christian authors, and by thus exposing my own past follies, hope it may stand as a beacon to my descendants, or others who may read it, to avoid them as a deadly poison, the destructive [sic] of eternal life, especially those works I have, by my own sad experience, proved to be pernicious; I mean, principally, Volney's moonshine theology, and Paine's delusive reasoning, but, without caution, the youthful, or those of riper years, the curious and thoughtless, alike, may be bitten by the infidel serpent. It is singular to be seen that, besides the many cross incidents in my military and civil life, there should be, in the most important part of it (my religion), some remarkable events. After all, it is for me to be thankful, and say with David, "O God, who is like unto thee? O what great troubles and adversities hast Thou shewed me, and yet didst Thou turn and refresh me: yea, Thou broughtest me from the deep of the earth again."[13] And again, I may well say with

9 Psalm 6:8.

10 Zechariah 3:2.

11 2 Corinthians 6:8.

12 A reference to John Bunyan's 1678 Christian allegory *The Pilgrim's Progress.*

13 Psalm 71:19-20.

him, "It is good for me that I have been in trouble, that I may learn thy statutes."[14] Yet I have more to be thankful for, that God has given me his influencing grace, and the means to enable me to keep my post in his happy service, fifteen years at St. Paul's, and, since that, six at St. Peter's, Walsall,[15] where I now attend, at the end of the year 1846.

The psalmist says, "We spend our years as a tale that is told."[16] It is true. Now, my years being so far spent, and my tale told, glancing at the retrospect, it affords no room for [con]gratulatory complacency, or any wish to spin my thread over again; and that, as my days are numbered, neither do I covet a lengthened period to their allotment, knowing that "Here we have no continuing city, but we seek one to come."[17] The feeble remnant I hope, in all sincerity, to devote to the service of God, faithful in his promises, simply relying on the merits of my Saviour; thereby looking for a joyful resurrection, trusting in his omnipotent power to save. So, until the signal is given, let my prayer be heard—"Lord, let me die the death of the righteous, and let my last end be like His."[18]

THE END.

14 Psalm 119:71.

15 St Peter's Church was erected in 1840. See Samuel Lewis, *A Topographical Dictionary of England* (London: Lewis and Co., seventh edition, 1848), vol. 4, p. 447.

16 Psalm 90:9.

17 Hebrews 13:14.

18 Numbers 23:10.

Epilogue

Little is known of Jackson's final years. He indeed moved to Birmingham in May 1847, as suggested in the closing paragraph of his narrative.[1] Thomas and his wife Elizabeth, aged 65 and 61 respectively, were living on Willis Street in Aston near Birmingham at the 1851 census.[2]

Thomas Jackson died at 47 Francis Street in Aston on 26 August 1859, aged 74, of 'Old age [and] chronic bronchitis'.[3]

1 See TNA, WO 23/35, Chelsea Registers, 1845-54, 1st-3rd Foot Guards.

2 Thomas Jackson was listed as a 'Chelsea Pensioner', while Elizabeth was noted as 'at home'. See TNA, HO 107/2061, St Matthew's Parish, Aston near Birmingham returns, p. 8.

3 TNA, WO 22/4, Chelsea Pension Returns, Birmingham District, and WO 23/46, Chelsea Registers, 1855-1866, Foot Guards to 10th Foot. Jackson was listed as an 'Out pensioner of Chelsea Hospital' on his death certificate, issued by the General Register Office. The informant present at the death was Mary Henshaw, resident at 46 Francis Street. She may well have been Jackson's daughter, Maria. See also French, *Thomas Jackson*, p. 27.

Index

From Reason to Revolution series – Warfare 1721-1815

http://www.helion.co.uk/published-by-helion/reason-to-revolution-1721-1815.html

The 'From Reason to Revolution' series covers the period of military history c. 1721–1815, an era in which fortress-based strategy and linear battles gave way to the nation-in-arms and the beginnings of total war.

This era saw the evolution and growth of light troops of all arms, and of increasingly flexible command systems to cope with the growing armies fielded by nations able to mobilise far greater proportions of their manpower than ever before. Many of these developments were fired by the great political upheavals of the era, with revolutions in America and France bringing about social change which in turn fed back into the military sphere as whole nations readied themselves for war. Only in the closing years of the period, as the reactionary powers began to regain the upper hand, did a military synthesis of the best of the old and the new become possible.

The series will examine the military and naval history of the period in a greater degree of detail than has hitherto been attempted, and has a very wide brief, with the intention of covering all aspects from the battles, campaigns, logistics, and tactics, to the personalities, armies, uniforms, and equipment.

Submissions

The publishers would be pleased to receive submissions for this series. Please contact series editor Andrew Bamford via email (andrewbamford18@gmail.com), or in writing to Helion & Company Limited, 26 Willow Road, Solihull, West Midlands, B91 1UE.

Titles

No 1 *Lobositz to Leuthen. Horace St Paul and the Campaigns of the Austrian Army in the Seven Years War 1756-57* Translated with additional materials by Neil Cogswell (ISBN 978-1-911096-67-2)

No 2 *Glories to Useless Heroism. The Seven Years War in North America from the French journals of Comte Maurés de Malartic, 1755-1760* William Raffle (ISBN 978-1-1911512-19-6) (paperback)

No 3 *Reminiscences 1808-1815 Under Wellington. The Peninsular and Waterloo Memoirs of William Hay* William Hay, with notes and commentary by Andrew Bamford (ISBN 978-1-1911512-32-5)

No 4 *Far Distant Ships. The Royal Navy and the Blockade of Brest 1793-1815* Quintin Barry (ISBN 978-1-1911512-14-1)

No 5 *Godoy's Army. Spanish Regiments and Uniforms from the Estado Militar of 1800* Charles Esdaile and Alan Perry (ISBN 978-1-911512-65-3) (paperback)

No 6 *On Gladsmuir Shall the Battle Be! The Battle of Prestonpans 1745* Arran Johnston (ISBN 978-1-911512-83-7)

No 7 *The French Army of the Orient 1798-1801. Napoleon's Beloved 'Egyptians'* Yves Martin (ISBN 978-1-911512-71-4)*

No 8 *The Autobiography, or Narrative of a Soldier. The Peninsular War Memoirs of William Brown of the 45th Foot* William Brown, with notes and commentary by Steve Brown (ISBN 978-1-911512-94-3) (paperback)

No 9 *Recollections from the Ranks. Three Russian Soldiers' Autobiographies from the Napoleonic Wars* Translated and annotated by Darrin Boland (ISBN 978-1-912174-18-8) (paperback)

No 10 *By Fire and Bayonet. Grey's West Indies Campaign of 1794* Steve Brown (ISBN 978-1-911512-60-8)

No 11 *Olmütz to Torgau. Horace St Paul and the Campaigns of the Austrian Army in the Seven Years War 1758-60* Translated with additional materials by Neil Cogswell (ISBN 978-1-911512-72-1)

No 12 *Murat's Army. The Army of the Kingdom of Naples 1806-1815* Digby Smith (ISBN 978-1-912390-09-0) (paperback)

No 13 *The Veteran or 40 Years' Service in the British Army. The Scurrilous Recollections of Paymaster John Harley 47th Foot – 1798-1838* John Harley, with notes and commentary by Gareth Glover (ISBN 978-1-912390-25-0) (paperback)

No 14 *Narrative of the Eventful Life of Thomas Jackson. Militiaman and Coldstream Sergeant, 1803-15* Thomas Jackson, with notes and commentary by Eamonn O'Keeffe (ISBN 978-1-912390-12-0) (paperback)

Books within this series are published in two major formats. 'Falconets' are paperbacks, page size 248mm × 180 mm, with high visual content including colour plates; 'Culverins' are hardback monographs, page size 234mm × 156mm. Books marked * in the list above are Falconets, all others are Culverins unless otherwise noted.